RONALD REAGAN WAS A BADASS:

Crazy But True Stories About
The United States' 40th President

BILL O'NEILL

ISBN: 978-1-64845-074-7

DON'T FORGET YOUR FREE BOOKS

TABLE OF CONTENTS

INTRODUCTION

Welcome to *Ronald Reagan Was a Badass: Some Truly Amazing Stories about the United States' Fortieth President*, a book that profiles the life and times of President Ronald Reagan, and shows how much of a badass he actually was! Ronald Reagan consistently polls as one of the United States' most popular post-World War II presidents, and historians generally agree that he was pretty effective, but often lost among those polls and studies is just how tough Ronnie really was and how that affected his presidency, the course of the United States, and the world.

This book was written to right that wrong.

Similar to many presidential biographies, this book will take you on a chronological journey through Ronald Reagan's life, from his boyhood in Illinois, to his career in Hollywood, and ultimately, his road to the Whitehouse. This book goes beyond a standard history book full of facts and dates. Sure, this book is jam-packed with true facts, but the emphasis is on Reagan's badassness and how that made him loved, respected, feared, and sometimes hated throughout the world. After all, what made Ronald Reagan a truly unique American president in many people's eyes, and part of the reason why he was so popular, was his rough and tough image. If John

Wayne had become president, he would have been like Ronald Reagan!

The book begins with Reagan's early life and career in Hollywood, where he played the role of a badass cowboy in several films and television shows. You'll also read about how Ronnie rose above one not-so-glamorous or badass role to still be successful.

You'll learn about how Reagan took on sometimes violent anti-war protesters when he was Governor of California, despite many of his advisors telling him not to do so. Reagan wasn't afraid to do his own thing and what he thought was right, even if it cost him some friends, allies, or even votes.

This book also chronicles how Reagan fought and won several tough political battles within the Republican Party on his way to win the presidential nomination and eventually the presidency.

But it wasn't until after Reagan became the United States' fortieth president that he put his full badassness on display for the world.

Many world leaders scoffed at Reagan's bold approach to geopolitics and American comedians and talk show hosts seemed to have never-ending source of material at the president's expense. They joked about his acting past, the fact that he still often dressed and acted like a cowboy, and his down-to-Earth way of speaking. Still, he persisted with his ideas to limit the size of the American government while trying to win the Cold War.

To fulfill his plans, Reagan had to use plenty of diplomacy to win the trust and respect of skeptical world leaders abroad and at home with the leaders of the Democrat Party, who controlled the House of Representatives during his presidency. In the end, the "cowboy president" was able to win the hearts and minds of many leaders and ordinary people, forging key alliances along the way, including with a badass pope and a badass female prime minister.

So, keep reading to learn about just how much of a badass Ronald Reagan was in 30 short stories that follow his life and times. At the end of every chapter there is a set of famous and memorable quotes said by Reagan that relate to the events just covered.

Sit back, relax, and enjoy learning about just how much of a badass America's fortieth president was!

CHAPTER 1

WIN JUST ONE
FOR THE GIPPER

The story of Ronald Wilson Reagan's career as a legendary badass president begins when the fortieth president was born on February 6, 1911, in the small town of Tampico, Illinois. Reagan spent most of his early years in the small north-central Illinois town of Dixon. For young Ronald, or "Dutch" as he was so often referred to due to his "Dutch-boy" haircut, life was slow, quiet, and easy.

Reagan was well-behaved at home and school. He took part in many post-curricular activities and brought home good grades. After high school, Reagan attended the 'Christian Eureka College' in Eureka, Illinois.

There was certainly nothing about Ronald Reagan's early life that would suggest he would later go on to become a legendary badass American president. Everything seemed to point toward the young man quietly settling down into some professional occupation, marrying, and having a family. Yes, Reagan was tall, athletic, well-spoken, intelligent, and ruggedly handsome, but so too were countless other American men.

And when Reagan graduated from Eureka in 1932, he was only interested in finding a job—any job—as the nation was in the midst of the Great Depression.

It was in that year that Reagan got the big break that set him on the course to stardom, power, and true badassness.

Reagan was offered a job with a Des Moines, Iowa radio station as the local announcer for Chicago Cubs games. Now, that might not seem like a very big deal, but it was fairly difficult for announcers back then, as they had to call the games via updates from the wire, not from streams, television, or even other radio broadcasts.

The young Illinoisan's strong and distinct voice made him popular with Iowa's Cubs' fans and eventually, he caught the attention of Warner Brothers Studios.

In 1937, Ronnie headed to Hollywood to show them just how much of a badass that a small-town boy from the Midwest could be.

Making His Mark on the Silver Screen

Reagan came up in Hollywood around the same time that John Wayne was starting to make his mark on the silver screen. I'd be the last person to try to convince you that Ronald Reagan was the equivalent of John Wayne in terms of acting, but an examination of Ronnie's career reveals that he showed many of his later badass tendencies as he struggled through Hollywood.

Hollywood has always been a tough place that chews up and spits outs actors as soon as they set foot in Tinseltown, especially those with few to no connections. For Reagan, even though he had a contract with Warner Brothers, he wasn't guaranteed very much. After all, he was just another bright-eyed kid from the Midwest—there were plenty more where he came from.

But Reagan persevered and built a nice little career doing bit parts and guest-starring roles in films, and after 1950, in television. Most of Reagan's roles were truly forgettable, but there were two parts he had that showed how much of a badass he could be, albeit in two very different ways.

Reagan played legendary Notre Dame University football player George "Gipper" Gipp in the 1940 film *Knute Rockne, All American*. Although the film was primarily about Notre Dame coach Knute Rockne, played by Pat O'Brien, Reagan stole a couple of scenes, especially the one where the ailing Gipp told Rockne to "win just one for the Gipper."

The line became famous almost as soon as Reagan uttered it. The scene became iconic, helping to launch Reagan's acting career and, in some ways, defining his later political career, as he became known as the "Big Gipper" after he became president.

Knute Rockne, All American certainly helped Reagan build a badass persona in Hollywood and later the political arena, but the future president also starred in a film that almost undid all of his efforts to be seen as a badass.

The 1951 film *Bedtime for Bonzo* had a plot that was as silly as its name, even in an era that was far less cynical and much more innocent than today. In the film, Reagan played a professor who attempted to teach a chimpanzee named Bonzo how to act more like a human. It was a 1950s version of a romantic comedy, but even then it was considered especially campy and cheesy.

It was Reagan's big chance to star in a leading role and, needless to say, it was also his last. Reagan's performance in *Bedtime for Bonzo* wasn't necessarily poor, but it just wasn't a good film and its campiness followed him well into his political career.

Still, Reagan did what all true badasses do by overcoming the setback. He continued to work in film and television well into the 1960s, partly because people remembered how badass he had been in *Knute Rockne, All American*, and despite the absolute silliness of *Bedtime for Bonzo*.

Hollywood Quotes

- "I didn't join up in this war to make money." – as John Hammond in *Desperate Journey* (1941).

- "In Hollywood, as I've often said, if you don't sing or dance, you end up as an after-dinner speaker." – quoted in his 1990 autobiography, *An American Life*.

- "Look, I might as well tell you now. He's a monkey." – as Peter Boyd in *Bedtime for Bonzo*.

- "How can a president not be an actor?" – Reagan said this somewhat sarcastically when asked if his acting career disqualified him from becoming president.

- "I approve of larceny; homicide is against my principles." – as gangster Jack Browning in his last film, the 1964 version of *The Killers*.

CHAPTER 2

REAGAN AND THE HUAC

As Ronald Reagan was making his name in Hollywood films during the 1940s and '50s, the Cold War was beginning and, along with it, the second Red Scare in the United States. Americans were genuinely concerned about a Soviet attack, but even more so, many believed that the attack would come from within. But, if there was one institution that was potentially filled with secret communists, it was Hollywood.

Hollywood and the American television industry have always been on the left wing of the political spectrum, so it was perhaps the perfect place for communists to infiltrate. The House Un-American Activities Committee (HUAC) began focusing on Hollywood and the American film and television industry as a potential target in late 1946, but it faced the problem of getting cooperative witnesses. Many in the film industry saw the HUAC as a witch hunt, while others were afraid to inform on people in the industry, ruining their chances to work in the process.

But then Ronnie came forward in 1947.

Taking a Not-So-Popular Stand against Communism in Hollywood

At the time, Reagan was president of the Screen Actors Guild (SAG) and therefore had a considerable amount of influence among his peers. He also had the kind of background knowledge the HUAC needed for its hearings. Still, Reagan was a bit reticent to testify against his colleagues and he wasn't necessarily a gung-ho anti-communist yet at that point in his life. Not to mention that the hearings were not very popular with many actors, writers, and directors in Hollywood. Reagan was actually a registered Democrat and considered himself to be a liberal when he testified at the HUAC.

Then his wife at the time, Jane Wyman, provided the influence to push Reagan into the realm of anti-communist politics.

Even in the 1940s, conservative Republicans were a rarity in Hollywood, but those who did exist, such as Wyman, were fairly influential as they had the HUAC and several important politicians in their corner.

The HUAC convened hearings in Washington in October 1947 about the influence of communism in Hollywood. Lauren Bacall, Humphrey Bogart, and dozens of other notable celebrities refused to take part in the hearings, leading some to be "blacklisted" for years and even decades. But among those who did testify were notable artist and director Walt Disney and B film actor and SAG president Ronald Reagan.

Reagan's testimony at the HUAC was nothing earth-shattering and was, for the most part. relegated to the back pages of the newspapers. Reagan stated that there was a possible communist influence in the SAG, but that the influence shouldn't be overstated.

Reagan also opposed banning political parties or groups based on their ideology.

Ronnie's testimony at the HUAC was more of a learning experience for the future American president than anything. He apparently learned that, if a man wanted to have a serious political career in the Cold War era, then he needed to be viewed as a badass defender of freedom.

And what better way to defend freedom than by fighting communism?

Reagan began his foray into anti-communist politics with baby steps in the late 1940s, but by the late 1960s, he was one of the most renowned anti-communists in America. It all began with his relationship to Jane Wyman, his presidency of SAG, and his love of freedom.

Quotes on Communism

- "How do you tell a communist? Well, it's someone who reads Marx and Lenin. And how do you tell an anti-Communist? It's someone who understands Marx and Lenin." (1982)

- "It was leadership here at home that gave us strong American influence abroad, and the collapse of imperial Communism." – at his 83rd birthday in 1994.

- "The years ahead will be great ones for our country, for the cause of freedom and the spread of civilization. The West will not contain Communism, it will transcend Communism." – excerpt from a 1981 Reagan speech.

- "I believe that communism is another sad, bizarre chapter in human history whose last pages even now are being written. I believe this because the source of our strength in the quest for human freedom is not material, but spiritual." – in a speech given to the National Association of Evangelicals in 1983.

- "The great dynamic success of capitalism had given us a powerful weapon in our battle against Communism—money." – excerpt from his autobiography, *Ronald Reagan: An American Life*.

CHAPTER 3

A BADASS ORATOR

If there is one thing that truly sent Ronald Reagan apart from the pack and ensured that he would rise to political greatness, it was his badass speaking and debating skills. Reagan had an uncanny ability to give a speech that could reassure the American people when the chips were down or even to fire them up if need be. Reagan also left his political opponents crying for mercy after debates.

There is no doubt that Ronald Reagan was a badass orator and perhaps one of the greatest among all American presidents, which is why he was given the nickname the "Great Communicator."

As we've already seen, Reagan's journey to being a badass orator and public speaker began in the 1930s when he was a radio announcer and continued after he began acting, but the future president's true transition into persuasive speech, and conservative politics, took place when he started hosting the *General Electric Theater* in 1954.

The General Electric Theater was a standard anthology radio and television show not unlike others of the era, but the position gave him a chance to give motivational speeches to General Electric employees around the country. Reagan wrote most his speeches, which focused on conservative ideas of anti-communism, free enterprise, and pro-church beliefs among other things; speeches which were supported and promoted by the conservative GE executives.

Still, Reagan felt he could do more, so he joined the Republican Party and quit acting in 1964 to dedicate his time to the pursuit of politics. Reagan became involved in Barry Goldwater's 1964 presidential campaign by delivering speeches for the candidate, and although Goldwater lost to Lyndon B. Johnson in a landslide, everyone remembered Reagan's badass speech titled "A Time for Choosing."

The speech ensured that Reagan would have a meteoric rise in American politics.

Speech and Debate Quotes

- "Those who deplore use of the terms 'pink' and 'leftist' are themselves guilty of branding all who oppose their liberalism as right wing extremists." – in "A Time for Choosing," October 27, 1964.

- "Reagan was a master at capturing a debate moment that everyone will remember." –

- Associated Press writer David Bauder in a 2008 article.

- "I will not make age an issue of this campaign. I am not going to exploit, for political purposes, my opponent's youth and inexperience." – during the 1984 presidential debates when asked if his age was a problem.

- "All must share in the productive work of this new beginning and all must share in the bounty of a revived economy, with the idealism and fair play which are the core of our system, and our strength, we can have a strong and prosperous America at peace with itself and the world." – at his first inaugural address on January 20, 1981.

- "The crew of the Space Shuttle *Challenger* honored us for the manner in which they lived their lives. We will never forget them, nor the last time we saw them, this morning, as they prepared for their journey and waved goodbye, and slipped the surly bonds of Earth to touch the face of God." – television address to the nation after the Space Shuttle *Challenger* disaster on January 28, 1986.

CHAPTER 4

REAGAN VS. THE HIPPIES

As much as Reagan's "A Time for Choosing" speech was truly badass, it didn't get Goldwater elected president. LBJ was just too much of a formidable opponent to beat, especially after the assassination of JFK, but the speech did establish Reagan as a legitimate player in Republican national politics and in the state of California.

You may be wondering how a Republican from California eventually went on to become America's fortieth president? Well, if Reagan had to run for office as a Republican in California's current political climate, then that alone would have made him an epic badass, but luckily for him, California was a very different place back then.

For the most part, California was politically conservative in the 1960s and majority Republican.

But San Francisco was pretty liberal even then and the college campuses were a hotbed of radical left-wing activity. The protests, riots, and even bombings and murders that were coming from a variety campus-orientated leftist groups became a priority for Reagan during the 1966 California's governor's election.

The Great Communicator expressed to the voters of California in no uncertain terms that, if elected, he was going to do everything in his power to stop the lawlessness coming from the college campuses, and the predominately older electorate responded by electing Reagan with over 57% of the vote.

Focusing on the Hotbed of Radical Activity

The Berkeley campus of the University of California was the center of the Free Speech Movement in the mid-1960s and by the time Reagan became governor, it had evolved to include many radicals who were not opposed to violence. Alongside legitimate and peaceful protesters were members of the Weather Underground, the Black Panthers, and Students for a Democratic Society (SDS). Reagan knew that, to break Berkeley's hold on the student protest movement, he had to change the university's leadership, which was sympathetic to the protests, and then go after the student leaders.

Once Reagan replaced several members of the University of California Board of Regents, he sent the California Highway Patrol into "People's Park," where the student protesters had gathered near the Berkeley campus.

On May 15, 1967, a day that later became known as "Bloody Thursday" by the protesters, the police dispersed the radicals by using a combination of buckshot and live shotgun rounds. One protester was killed and hundreds of protesters and police were wounded in the ensuing riot.

Once the smoke cleared — literally — Reagan sent the National Guard into Berkeley to keep the peace. Although student protests continued and the faculty of Berkeley for the most part continued to support the radical students, Reagan's popularity wasn't hurt in the least by the violence. Just as a true badass would do, Reagan made no apologies for the violence and said that it was needed to keep order.

The voters of California showed their assent by re-electing Ronnie in 1970.

Quotes on Government and Hippies

- "Government exists to protect us from each other. Where government has gone beyond its limits is in deciding to protect us from ourselves."

- "As government expands, liberty contracts." – as quoted by Michael Reagan in *The Last Best Hope: The Greatest Speeches of Ronald Reagan*.

- "A hippie is someone who looks like Tarzan, walks like Jane, and smells like Cheetah."

- "Government is like a baby. An alimentary canal with a big appetite at one end and no sense of responsibility on the other." – as quoted by Bill Adler in *The Reagan Wit: The Humor of the American President*.

- "The vast majority of students at the university only wanted an education. But for months they were robbed of it by the rampaging of a minority." – quote about the Berkeley, California protests.

CHAPTER 5

RONNIE AND THE DEATH PENALTY

One of the major things that made Ronald Reagan so popular and such a badass in many people's eyes was how he approached the problems of the time: simple, straight ahead, and without fanfare. Reagan was no intellectual in the sense that he never used a complex lexicon and he never talked above people in terms that only university-educated academics would understand. He knew what appealed to most Americans and what their hopes and fears were.

And in the 1960s, especially in California, most Americans feared the growing instability.

The War in Vietnam, domestic terrorism, and campus unrest were all issues that people had opinions about, but nearly all Americans at the time, regardless of their political affiliations, agreed that crime was truly out of hand. The saying "history repeats itself" is often overused and usually misunderstood, but when it comes to comparing the present-day United States with that of the late 1960's, there are certainly many parallels. Besides the political unrest, crime was rampant in the late

1960's; it was so bad that some US cities more closely resembled a Philip K. Dick story than 1950's America.

Getting Tough on Crime

Reagan knew that there was great anxiety over the skyrocketing crime rate, so along with his promise to get tough on leftist militants, he promised to get tough on crime in California.

Reagan argued that part of the reason that the crime rate was soaring was that criminals just weren't serving enough time when sentenced. Once elected governor, Reagan pushed for longer sentences for criminals, especially those convicted of violent crimes, and he promised to use the death penalty for the most egregious of all crimes.

On April 11, 1967, cop killer Aaron Mitchel was executed by gas chamber in San Quentin, making him the first and only prisoner to be executed on Reagan's watch. Far from being bloodthirsty, Reagan granted one death row inmate clemency as he believed the evidence was too thin to warrant a death sentence. Still, Reagan planned to keep his promise by allowing more executions to proceed, but the California Supreme Court stopped all executions in its 1972 *People v. Anderson* decision.

The decision meant that everyone sentenced to death before the decision was given life sentences. Among those who were given a second chance were Charles Manson and Bobby Kennedy's assassin, Sirhan Sirhan.

Despite the setback, Reagan continued to support law and order through his two terms as California governor by signing laws that gave more money to California's police departments and prisons. Most Californians at the time agreed with Reagan's views on law and order and more and more people around the country were beginning to hear about the badass governor from the Golden State.

They liked what they heard and were willing to hear more.

Quotes on Law and Order

- "I urge the House to follow the Senate and enact proposals permitting use of all reliable evidence that police offices acquire in good faith. These proposals would also reform the habeas corpus laws and allow, in keeping with the will of the overwhelming majority of Americans, the use of the death penalty where necessary." – at his 1985 "State of the Union Address."

- "Let us not forget who we are. Drug abuse is a repudiation of everything America is."

- "Governor thanks for saving my life. . . I run a liquor store. Last week, a thug broke in. He intended to rob us, but I resisted him. He wrestled me to the floor and poised his knife about my throat. I shouted out, 'Go ahead and kill me! You'll get the death penalty and be executed, just like the guy last week." – letter from California resident to Governor Ronald Reagan thanking him for supporting capital punishment in the state.

- "You pointed out that the police would be so busy arresting handgun owners that they would be unable to protect the people against criminals. It's a nasty truth, but those who seek to inflict harm are not fazed by gun control laws. I happen to know this from personal experience." – speech to the National Rifle Association in 1983.

- "We fought a war on poverty, and poverty won."

CHAPTER 6

NOT QUITE BADASS ENOUGH IN 1976

The thing that many historical badasses have in common—whether they were badass generals, politicians, artists, or even outlaws—is a healthy dose of ambition. In that respect, Ronald Reagan was no different. Reagan strove to rise to the top of whatever profession he was in and by the early 1970s, many in the Republican Party were mentioning him as a potential presidential candidate.

Reagan had the popular appeal, he was polished and media savvy, and perhaps most importantly, he could win the electoral rich state of California. But President Richard Nixon was riding a wave of relative popularity after his re-election in 1972, so Reagan would have to wait until 1976 or later for his presidential run.

Then along came the Watergate scandal.

Nixon's role and/or knowledge of the Watergate break-in led to his resignation and passing of the mantle of the presidency to Vice President Gerald Ford, who had replaced Nixon's original vice president, Spiro Agnew, another resignation due to the Watergate scandal. Ford initially came into office with plenty of goodwill from the American people, but after he pardoned Nixon, things quickly unraveled. Then the economy took a nosedive and things were looking pretty bleak during America's bicentennial.

A Chance for Greatness?

So, Governor Reagan stepped up to show what a badass he was by doing something almost unheard of in American history: challenging a sitting president in a presidential primary. It would be an almost impossible task to pull off, but if anyone could do it, it was Reagan.

Ford was supported by the Republican Party establishment and the finance/business wing of the party, while Reagan's followers were younger and much more socially conservative. It would be a tight and at times bitter primary fight that was echoed in many ways in the 2016 presidential primaries in both major parties.

Ford started the primaries by winning New Hampshire and several other states, but Reagan picked up some key endorsements in the south. By the time the 1976 Republican National Convention rolled around in August, Reagan had won most of the South and almost the entire West, while Ford dominated in the Northeast. The two candidates split the Midwest.

Ford was ahead on the delegate votes going into the convention, but he was short of the number needed to claim an outright victory. The delegates voted again, and after some crafty maneuvering by Ford and a costly mistake by Reagan, Ford was declared the winner.

If Reagan had succeeded in unseating Ford in the primaries or convention it would have been a truly epic badass move. He nearly did it, which was pretty badass itself, but Ronnie wouldn't have to wait long to have another chance at the highest office in the land.

Quotes on Politics

- "Republicans believe every day is the Fourth of July, but the Democrats believe every day is April 15."

- "Politics is not a bad profession. If you succeed there are many rewards, if you disgrace yourself you can always write a book."

- "Socialism only works in two places: Heaven where they don't need it and hell there they already have it."

- "The trouble with our liberal friends is not that they're ignorant. It's just that they know so much that isn't so."

- "You and I are told increasingly that we have to choose between a left or a right. There is only an up or down: up to man's age-old dream—the ultimate in individual freedom consistent with law and order—or down to the ant heap of totalitarianism. And regardless of their sincerity, their humanitarian motives, those who would trade our freedom for security have embarked on this downward course." – 1964 speech "A Time for Choosing."

CHAPTER 7

BADASS ENOUGH TO WHIP THE PEANUT FARMER

Losing the 1976 Republican presidential nomination was a tough pill to swallow for Reagan. Unlike most politicians, he was a winner from the beginning and started with a relatively high-profile office as the governor of California. But losing the 1976 Republican presidential nomination was a blessing in disguise for Ronnie.

Due to the lagging economy, the American people were ready for a change and Georgia Governor and peanut farmer Jimmy Carter seemed like just the man to turn things around and bring the country together. Carter's affable nature and almost soft-spoken tone were a direct contrast to the often brash nature of Nixon and his men, of which Ford was one. Ford just didn't seem to have it together to get the job done.

America voted overwhelmingly in the electoral college and popular vote for Carter.

But it soon became apparent that Carter too, didn't have it together and was probably in over his head. Although the US was technically out of recession by 1975, the economy continued to lag with slow job growth. The crime wave of the

1960s continued well into the 1970s and was so bad in some cities that there was a major exodus to the suburbs. New York City, for example, was routinely found to be one of the most unsafe American cities by many metrics.

And as all of this was happening, the Islamic Revolution took place in Iran in 1978, culminating with militants taking over the American embassy and holding 52 Americans hostage.

To most Americans, Jimmy Carter seemed like a nice guy, but nice guys just don't cut it in times such as those. America needed a badass!

Ronnie to the Rescue

Reagan ran again for the Republican Party's presidential nomination in 1980, but now he was better organized, was known nationally, and was able to take advantage of a weak Republican field. Reagan won the nomination during the primaries more than a month before the convention, which gave him extra time to pick a running mate and to plan his attack on Ford.

Ronnie selected former CIA director and establishment Republican George H. W. Bush as his running mate, but by October, it looked like it wouldn't matter as the polls had Carter far out front.

Then came the debates.

Although there were technically two debates, Carter only showed up for the second one on October 28. Third-party candidate John Anderson and Regan debated in the first one on September 21. After Carter was done with the October 28 debate, he probably thought he should have skipped that one too. The Great Communicator talked circles around the peanut farmer, showing what a badass orator and debater he was, uttering the famous lines, "there you go again," when Carter accused him of wanting to eliminate Medicare.

When Americans finally went to the polls on November 4, 1980, it wasn't even close. Reagan won just over 50% of the vote to Carter's 41% and Anderson's 6.6%. But even more important was the electoral vote count, which is how American presidential elections are decided. Reagan won 489 to 49 in one of the greatest electoral college landslides in history.

Winning the presidency was a true test of Reagan's badass nature, but he would soon find himself facing even bigger challenges.

Economics Quotes

- "The Democrats in the legislature agreed with us that welfare costs were headed for the stratosphere but claimed the solution was a huge tax increase—in other words, to keep pouring more money into a bucket that was full of holes." – in his 1990 autobiography, *Ronald Reagan: An American Life.*

- "As I have often said, governments don't produce economic growth, people do." – in his 1990 autobiography, *Ronald Reagan: An American Life.*

- "What of all the entrepreneurs that fail? Well, many do, particularly the successful ones; often several times. And if you ask them the secret of their success, they'll tell you it's all that they learned in their struggles along the way; yes, it's what they learned from failing." – in his 1990 autobiography, *Ronald Reagan: An American Life.*

- "We should measure welfare's success by how many people leave welfare, not by how many are added."

- "There's a woman in Chicago. She has 80 names, 30 addresses, 12 Social Security cards and is collecting veterans' benefits on four non-existent deceased husbands. She's got Medicaid, is getting food stamps and welfare under each of her names. Her tax-free cash income alone is over $150,000." – in a speech during the 1976 Republican presidential primaries on real-life con-artist Linda Taylor.

CHAPTER 8

AGE WASN'T A PROBLEM FOR REAGAN

Modern politics is not for the weak of heart. Men and women who decide to enter the cutthroat arena of politics have to have thick skin, steel resolve, and the vigor of a young person. Since most young people don't have the experience, maturity, or connections to make it in politics, the profession has been left to women and men who have the vigor but tend to be in middle age. Although successful American politicians have historically not been young, they also haven't been very old either.

The United States Constitution requires that the president be at least 35-years-old, but there isn't any maximum age requirement. With that said, the average age of American president upon assuming office is 55-years-old. So, when Reagan became Governor of California at the age of 56, he was already a late bloomer in politics.

Many thought that Reagan was just too old to be president and when the 1980 election rolled around, he was 69, which many believed was too advanced in age. When Reagan was inaugurated, he became the oldest man to assume the office, this record held until 2017 when Donald Trump was inaugurated at the age of 70.

Interestingly, Jimmy Carter didn't make much of a big deal about Reagan's age, although it was later brought up by a moderator during one of the 1984 presidential debates. After being asked if his then age of 73 was a problem, the Great Communicator replied in typical fashion.

> "I want you to know also I will not make age an issue of this campaign. I am not going to exploit for political purposes my opponent's youth and inexperience."

The quote was a hit with the public, demonstrating that badasses can be any age.

Religious and Spiritual Quotes

- "America was founded by people who believe that God was their rock of safety."

- "I have wondered at times about what the Ten Commandments would have looked like if Moses had run them through the US Congress."

- "If we ever forget that we're one nation under God, then we will be a nation gone under."

- "Evil is powerless if the good are unafraid."

- "We are never defeated unless we give up on God."

CHAPTER 9

DIVORCE WASN'T A PROBLEM EITHER

Ronnie proved that, despite being a bit long in the tooth, he was still a badass and capable of governing the Western world's most powerful nation. Age is often related to virility, or at least the perception of it, but Reagan didn't have any control over it, other than proving to the American people that he was healthy and virile. After jumping that hurdle, though, Reagan faced another potential social obstacle during his 1980 presidential run—his divorce from actress Jane Wyman.

The impact that the divorce played in the 1980 presidential election is not fully known, but few will argue that it played no role at all. "No-fault" divorce had just been legalized in California in 1970, signed into law by then-Governor Ronald Reagan. After no-fault divorce was legalized nationwide, divorce rates sharply shot up in the 1970s until nearly half of all newly married couples later divorced. You could say that divorce had become quite popular by 1980.

With that said, Americans still like their presidents to represent a higher moral standard.

Divorcees had run for the highest office before 1980, the most notable being Democrat Illinois Governor Adlai Stevenson II. Stevenson already had a tough battle to begin with, going up against World War II hero Dwight Eisenhower, but then his divorce also became an issue that wouldn't go away. A divorcee didn't run again for the presidency until Reagan.

In the years after Stevenson, the US had elected its first Catholic president, which was once thought to be taboo as well, so it appeared ready to elect its first divorcee in 1980. The surge in divorces in the 1970s didn't discriminate: Americans of all races, religions, economic backgrounds, and political parties found themselves divorcing in never before seen numbers. Divorce was something that everyone could relate to and, in some ways, it became another factor that made Reagan more relatable.

What was once a political liability very well may have helped Reagan pick up some middle-of-the-road voters in 1980.

Quotes on Social Issues

- "I've noticed that everybody that is for abortion has already been born." - response at the September 21, 1980, presidential debate against John Anderson.

- "Some women just aren't the marrying kind — or, anyway, not the permanent marrying kind, and I'm one of them." - actress Jane Wyman on her marriage and divorce to Reagan and her general feelings about the institution of marriage.

- "My personal belief is that God couldn't create evil, so the desires he planted in us are good and the physical relationship between a man and a woman is the highest form of companionship." - a 1951 letter to a female friend who had just divorced and planned to never again marry.

- "Families stand at the center of our society. And every family has a personal stake in promoting excellence in education."

- "Morality in the long run aligned with strategy." - on his long-range plans while in office.

CHAPTER 10

BULLETPROOF RONNIE

Reagan's first term as president began with a lot of optimism but was pretty uneventful for the first two months. Then on March 20, 1981, at 2:27 p.m., Reagan had a chance to prove just how much of a badass he was to the world when a crazed gunman named John Hinkley Junior shot the president with a .22 caliber gun. Although the caliber is small and Reagan was only hit once, it bounced around the insides of the president's body and lodged inside his lung.

It was touch and go for a while, and the incident nearly threw the government into a constitutional crisis.

Hinkley was a privileged but unhinged individual. It was later revealed that he committed the act to impress Jodie Foster (the actress), whom he was obsessed with, but thankfully, he didn't know what target practice was.

As Reagan was leaving the Washington Hilton after a meeting with labor leaders, Hinkley took advantage of a brief lapse in security and was able to fire six shots. One shot hit White House Press Secretary James Brady in the head, giving him permanent brain damage, although he lived to 2014. Another shot hit District of Columbia Metro Police officer Thomas Delahanty, who is still alive. Labor leader Alfred Antenucci then attempted to grab Hinckley, forcing the gunman to fire the rest of the shots wildly. Secret Service Agent Tim McCarthy then intentionally absorbed one shot, with the final shot hitting the president's limousine.

The shot ricocheted and went into the president.

The Fight of His Life

Reagan was in for the fight of his life. The tough political fights he had been in, in California and on the road to the Whitehouse, probably helped prepare him psychologically for this. Taking a bullet in the lung was something that only a true badass could survive.

The president was then brought down the street to George Washington University Hospital for surgery. Although Ronnie was in great pain and bleeding internally, he insisted on walking from the limo to the operating room. Needless to say, everyone there was impressed with the president's grit.

Many people didn't think Reagan would live. In reality, most 70-year-olds wouldn't live through a similar situation, but Ronnie was in excellent health for his age, he was stubborn, and most importantly, he was a well-seasoned badass by that point in his life. And once his wife Nancy arrived at the hospital, his spirits seemed to pick up more, and he made numerous jokes to the doctors, nurses, and his staff. After undergoing a risky operation on his chest that lasted more than an hour and a half, Reagan was in recovery, but he wasn't out of the woods.

After recovering in the hospital for nearly two weeks, Ronnie and Nancy finally emerged on the morning of April 11. To those watching at home on TV, it was clear that Reagan was moving a little slower than usual, but he looked otherwise good. For many Americans, it seemed as though it was a miracle.

It took several months for Reagan to fully get back to his pre-injury self. Still, how many of us could take a bullet in the lungs and be up and running the country again within a couple of weeks? As tragic as the shooting was, and as truly terrible as it could have been, it ended up having a positive effect on Reagan's image and the overall American population.

Reagan's approval rating shot up to an unheard of 73% after the shooting, and most Americans were more united as well. The attempted assassination not only cemented Reagan's reputation as a badass, in no time he became a symbol of American strength in many people's eyes.

Quotes about His Attempted Assassination and His Duties as President

- "Honey, I forgot to duck." – to wife Nancy when she arrived at the hospital.

- "I hope you're all Republicans." – to his doctors just before surgery.

- "Today, Mr. President, we are all Republicans." – lead surgeon Joseph Giordano just before the surgery.

- "All in all, I'd rather be in Philadelphia." – note written by Reagan for one of his nurses before surgery.

- "I've laid down the law, though, to everyone from now on about anything that happens: no matter what time it is, wake me, even if it's in the middle of a Cabinet meeting." –when asked about decision making during emergencies, such as his attempted assassination.

CHAPTER 11

SANDRA DAY O'CONNOR

One of the qualities of a true badass is a fearlessness to make decisions that may not seem popular at the time with one's peers. For Reagan, one of these decisions involved a choice that at first seemed controversial to many of his conservative peers but was quickly championed by all and became a sort of rallying point.

While on the campaign trail in 1980, Reagan addressed several issues that the Republican base and all voters of America believed were important. Reagan continually referred to the dismal economy and the Soviet Union (we'll get to both of those in a bit) and his background as a divorced former Hollywood actor. He did well with all of those issues, but the polls showed that he was lagging considerably behind Carter with women. The Carter campaign played up this perception by portraying Reagan as a dinosaur from another era when those like him were happy with women being kept in the home.

Reagan's campaign advisors knew he had to do something, but whatever he did, he couldn't appear to pander to the feminists. For the most part, conservatives detested feminists, and Reagan's advisors knew that he would never get the feminist vote regardless.

So, Ronnie had to walk another tight rope to cut into Carter's lead with women.

Reagan announced that, if elected president, he would appoint a woman to the United States Supreme Court.

She Was No Feminist

Sandra Day O'Connor was born into a Texas ranching family and grew up in rural Arizona. Due to her rural background, Sandra learned self-sufficiency at an early age, which translated into her being accepted into the prestigious Stanford University and after graduation attending Stanford Law School.

Day's (her maiden name) attendance and good marks at Stanford may not seem like that big a deal today, but it's important to know that she did all that, and got married, in the early 1950s when most American women were expected to concentrate on making a home.

O'Connor went on to work as a lawyer, raised three children, and became involved in Republican Party politics in the Phoenix, Arizona area. She then went on to serve as Arizona's attorney general for a term, was the majority leader in the Arizona Senate, and was a judge in the Arizona State Court of Appeals.

In other words, Sandra Day O'Connor was a bit of a badass in her own right!

Well, being from out West, Reagan was quite familiar with Day O'Connor's career, so for him, it was an obvious choice to nominate her for the Supreme Court. Of course, there were those in the Republican Party who weren't very receptive to

43

the idea of a woman serving on the nation's highest court, but after Ronnie won the election, he used his charm and some wheeling and dealing to win them over.

Reagan nominated Sandra Day O'Connor on August 19, 1981, and on September 21 the Senate confirmed her by a vote of 99 to 0.

Some of Reagan's political opponents later claimed that his nomination of Sandra Day O'Connor was little more than a cynical political move—he knew that the Democrats would never oppose the first female Supreme Court justice and in the process, he would win a notable political battle.

Well, if that's the case, it's just another example of Reagan being a badass.

QUOTES ON HISTORY

- "You and I know and do not believe that life is so dear and peace so sweet as to be purchased at the price of chains and slavery. If nothing in life is worth dying for, when did this begin—just in the face of this enemy? Or should Moses have told the children of Israel to live in slavery under the pharaohs? Should Christ have refused the cross? Should the patriots at Concord Bridge have thrown down their guns and refused to fire the shot heard 'round the world?" – in *Speaking My Mind: Selected Speeches with Personal Reflections.*

- "James Madison said in 1788: 'Since the general civilization of mankind, I believe there are more instances of the abridgement of the freedom of the people by gradual and silent encroachment of those in power than by violent and sudden usurpations." – in *Ronald Reagan: An American Life.*

- "Democracy triumphed in the Cold War because it was a battle of values—between one system that gave preeminence to the state and another that gave preeminence to the individual and freedom." – in *Ronald Reagan: An American Life.*

- "History is made by men and women of vision and courage. Tonight freedom is on the march." – at the February 4, 1986 State of the Union Address.

- "Great nations which fail to meet their responsibilities are consigned to the dust bin of history. We grew from that small, weak republic which had as its assets spirit, optimism, faith in God and an unshakeable belief that free men and women could govern themselves wisely. We became the leader of the free world, an example of all those who cherish freedom."

CHAPTER 12

BEHIND EVERY BADASS . . .

You've probably heard the saying, "Behind every good man is a good/strong woman." Well, this aphorism is true for badasses as well, as we can see with the life and times of Ronald Reagan. As Reagan made his meteoric rise through the American political system and government, behind him every step of the way was his wife Nancy. The media sometimes gave Nancy a hard time for her belief in astrology and her "Just Say No" campaign to reduce illicit drug and alcohol use by American youths, but the reality is she was smart, capable, and a true trend-setter. Unlike most of her predecessors, Nancy Reagan was a very active, public first lady who always supported her husband.

Nancy Davis met Ronald Reagan in Hollywood in the early 1950s, as she struggled to make a name for herself in minor film and television roles, even starring opposite Ronnie in episodes of the Westerns *Wagon Train* and *The Tall Man*.

But Nancy's most important work would come in supporting her husband's political ambitions.

She was with him every step of the way, from his campaign for California governor to his last days in the White House, always offering Ronnie advice when asked but never unsolicited. The couple had a deep love and respect for each other, with Nancy giving Ronald the nickname "Ronnie" and Ronald in turn calling her "Mommie."

Like Ronnie, the former actress was extremely photogenic, well-spoken, and physically attractive. Long before Melania Trump awed fashion fans with her stylish clothing, Nancy Reagan brought high fashion and design to the White House. By the mid-1980s, few people in America could say a bad word about Nancy, not even Ronnie's fiercest critics.

The War on Drugs

Reagan took his "get tough on crime stance" as governor with him to the White House. It was one of the things that helped him get elected president, so he was serious about following through with his pledge in his first term. Crime was still rising in 1980 and many of America's cities were having major problems, which gave Reagan the support to push major crime bills through Congress.

The Democrat-controlled Congress passed the Comprehensive Crime Control Act of 1984 , the Anti-Drug Abuse Act of 1986, and the Anti-Drug Abuse Act of 1988, which were signed into law by Reagan, as part of the "War on Drugs."

The term "War on Drugs" was first coined by President Richard Nixon in the early 1970s, and it wasn't always popular. Many minority communities believe the War on Drugs unfairly targeted them, and many civil libertarians thought that the laws were draconian and an abuse of police and government power.

Still, the new laws seemed to be working, because by 1983, the crime rate was dropping in the United States.

Always the political badass who was thinking at least two moves ahead of his opponents, Reagan employed his attractive and popular wife to help with the mission. Nancy was going to reduce America's youth drug problem by getting them to 'Just Say No.'

Those three simple words became a badass public relations campaign that raised Nancy's public profile, probably helped Ronnie get re-elected, and became a major part of American pop culture in the 1980s. If you were a kid growing up in the 1980s, you couldn't avoid the 'Just Say No' campaign. It was in public service announcements during your favorite cartoons, special Just Say No comic books and other merchandise were given away at schools, and it became a theme of many sitcoms and television shows of the era. Nancy even made a guest appearance on the hit show *Diff'rent Strokes* and other shows to promote 'Just Say No' and also made public appearances with actor and celebrity tough guy Mr. T.

Experts have debated whether or not the 'Just Say No' campaign reduced youth drug and alcohol use in America, but there no doubt that by leading the campaign, Nancy Reagan helped her husband.

Humorous Reagan Quotes

- "Politics is supposed to be the second-oldest profession. I have come to realize that it bears a very close resemblance to the first."

- "Where the preservation of a natural resource like the redwoods is concerned, that there is a common sense limit. I mean, if you've looked at a hundred thousand acres or so of trees—you know, a tree is a tree, how many more do you need to look at?" – when asked about the conflict between environmentalists and loggers in California.

- "Here's my strategy on the Cold War: We win, they lose." – in answer to a reporter when asked how the US would win the Cold War.

- "My fellow Americans. I'm pleased to announce that I've signed legislation outlawing the Soviet Union. We begin bombing in five minutes." – during a "hot mic" moment on August 11, 1984 before a scheduled radio address.

- "Status quo, you know, is Latin for 'the mess we're in'."

CHAPTER 13

NOT AFRAID OF
THE EVIL EMPIRE

Once Reagan was inaugurated and officially became the President of the United States of America, just about everyone in the world understood there was a new sheriff in town. The Ayatollah Khomeini, the leader of the Iranian Islamic Revolution who became the head of the Islamic Republic of Iran, knew that Reagan was a different sort of leader to his predecessor.

The American hostages held by radical students in Iran were released on January 20, 1981, just minutes after Reagan ended his inaugural speech. Needless to say, most don't believe the timing was coincidental.

In some ways, Reagan and his predecessor Jimmy Carter were similar. They were both down-to-Earth, affable guys who embodied American qualities and values. They were both success stories who earned that success through a combination of intelligence and plenty of hard work. Both were self-made men. But Carter was seen by many as *too* nice and Reagan was, well...he was rightfully viewed as a badass.

Almost as soon as he took office, Reagan made it his goal to confront head-on what he saw as the primary enemy of the United States and the West.

Confronting Freedom's Enemies

Historically epic badasses have always had something higher that drove them to be badasses. Whether it was a higher ideal or belief system, the love of one's people, or even pure greed, a true badass always has an unquenchable desire to fight for that greater thing. Reagan was driven by his desire to preserve what he believed was an ideal America, while at the same time confronting what he thought was the evilest system on Earth at the time — communism.

For Reagan, communism wasn't just some abstract concept that radicals in coffee shops talked about, nor was it something on the other side of the world that posed no threat to America. No, Reagan saw communism as an existential threat to the American way of life and if there was any way he could stop it, he would.

And Soviet Union leader Yuri Andropov also knew this.

Ideologically speaking, Andropov was a mirror image of Reagan in many ways. He was a former KGB officer, a communist ideologue, and a true patriot of the Soviet state. Andropov was also a bit of a badass in his own right, helping to suppress the 1954 Hungarian Uprising and the 1968 Prague Spring when he worked for the KGB.

So, when Andropov became the head of the USSR in 1982, he knew what type of opponent he faced in Reagan. Andropov immediately ordered the Soviet military to conduct military maneuvers with its Eastern European allies in the Warsaw Pact and brought back the tradition of military parades through Red Square in Moscow.

None of that scared Reagan, though.

All of Andropov's military and ideological posturing only seemed to make Reagan more determined and also seemed to prove what he had been arguing all the time—that communism in general and the Soviet Union, in particular, were intent on dominating the world.

But Reagan knew that turning the Cold War hot would mean everyone would lose, so he decided to fight the Soviet Union and communism with his best weapon: his speaking abilities.

With the help of his speechwriter, Anthony Dolan, Reagan delivered two badass speeches that indicted the Soviet Union and set the tone for the end of the Cold War. The first speech, delivered by Reagan to the British House of Commons on June 8, 1982, became known as the "Ash Heap of History" speech because he stated that "freedom and democracy will leave Marxism and Leninism on the ash heap of history."

The speech that solidified Ronnie's bona fides as a legitimate anti-communist badass was his "Evil Empire" speech, which he delivered to the National Association of Evangelicals on March 8, 1983. In that speech, Reagan stated about the Soviet Union:

> "The temptation of blithely declaring yourselves above it all and label both sides equally at fault, to ignore the facts of history and the aggressive impulses of an *evil empire*, to

simply call the arms race a giant misunderstanding and thereby remove yourself from the struggle between right and wrong and good and evil."

The speech caused quite a ruckus in both the West and the East. Many of Reagan's critics in the US and other Western nations thought that it was too provocative and that it unnecessarily stirred up emotions that could potentially lead to war.

But to Andropov, the Soviets, and the rest of the communist world, for that matter, it was clear that Reagan wasn't messing around. It was obvious that Reagan was no Jimmy Carter and that he very well could be a badass cowboy, just like many of the characters he had played.

Quotes on Communism

- "During my first press conference as president, in answer to a direct question, I pointed out that, as good Marxist-Leninists, the Soviet leaders have openly and publicly declared that the only morality they recognize is that which will further their cause, which is world revolution. I think I should point out I was only quoting Lenin, their guiding spirit, who said in 1920 that they repudiate all morality that proceeds from supernatural ideas–that's their name for religion–or ideas that are outside class conceptions. Morality is entirely subordinate to the interests of class war. And everything is moral that is necessary for the annihilation of the old exploiting social order and for uniting the proletariat." – from the "Evil Empire" speech on March 8, 1983.

- "The strength of the Solidarity movement in Poland demonstrates the truth told in an underground joke in the Soviet Union. It is that the Soviet Union would remain a one-party nation even if an opposition party were permitted, because everyone would join the opposition party." – from the "Ash Heap of History" speech on June 8, 1982.

- "Socialists ignore the side of man that is the spirit. They can provide you shelter, fill your belly with bacon and beans, treat you when you're ill, all the things guaranteed to a prisoner or a slave. They don't understand that we also dream."

- "I would agree to a freeze if only we could freeze the Soviets' global desires. A freeze at current levels of weapons would remove any incentive for the Soviets to negotiate seriously in Geneva and virtually end our chances to achieve the major arms reductions which we have proposed. Instead, they would achieve their objectives through the freeze." – from the "Evil Empire" speech on March 8, 1983.

- "Wherever the comparisons have been made between free and closed societies—West Germany and East Germany, Austria and Czechoslovakia, Malaysia and Vietnam—it is the democratic countries that are prosperous and responsive to the needs of their people. And one of the simple but overwhelming facts of our time is this: Of all the millions of refugees we've seen in the modern world, their flight is always away from, not toward the communist world." – from the "Ash Heap of History" speech on June 8, 1982.

CHAPTER 14

THE COWBOY IN CHIEF

For all American presidents, a carefully-crafted image, especially in the years after World War II when television became such a big part of society, has been vital to success. Most presidents want to appeal to the broadest slice of society as possible, but when that isn't possible, they at least try to appeal to their dedicated base of support. Woodrow Wilson presented the image of a thoughtful intellectual, while John F. Kennedy was more of an inspiring sort of guy.

Ronald Reagan's image was that of a badass cowboy.

Since Reagan had acted in many Western films and television shows, the image of him wearing a cowboy hat and riding on a horse stuck with him through his time as governor and well into his presidency. It was an image that many of his political enemies, and much of the press, attempted to use against him by portraying him as an out of touch buffoon from an era that was best left dead. The foreign media also loved to portray Reagan as a literal cowboy who could quite possibly bring about World War III.

But in true badass style, Reagan seemed to relish the image and played it up for propaganda purposes. Sure, he legitimately seemed to enjoy the Western US and its culture and history, but he was also partially trolling the media and building an image that Americans could identify with—that of a strong, "Marlboro man" figure.

The Western Whitehouse

When Reagan was on the campaign trail or doing his business in Sacramento as governor or Washington as president, he was all business and dressed like standard politician, but when he was at his sprawling ranch compound known as "Rancho del Cielo" near Santa Barbara, California, he was 100% cowboy.

For Reagan, Rancho del Cielo was a place where he, Nancy, their children, and their extended family and friends could spend quality time far away from the gaze of the press.

But sometimes, Ronnie *wanted* the press to gaze on him, even at Rancho del Cielo.

The Reagans purchased the ranch in 1974 when Ronnie was governor for the high price at the time of $527,000. The Reagans visited the ranch 40 times during his terms as president for an average of about 50 days per year, but it was far from a vacation pad for the president.

Reagan often invited foreign dignitaries as well as American politicians to the ranch to conduct business, earning it the title the "Western White House." Even when he wasn't doing official business at the ranch, Ronnie enjoyed doing tough, cowboy work, such as building fences, pruning trees, and building additions himself.

As much as Reagan may have loved Rancho del Cielo as a place to escape the press, he also knew how to use the press to foster his image. Whenever the press was at the ranch, Ronnie made sure to wear a cowboy hat, boots, and to ride a horse. It may have been contrived and a bit silly, but most people seemed to love it—and those who didn't still talked about it.

After all, most Americans in the 1980s had grown up with Westerns on the television so, to them, nothing could be more badass than a cowboy president!

Quotes on Culture

- "It is true that I opposed quotas in employment, education, and other areas. I consider quotas, whether they favor blacks or whites, men or women, to be a new form of discrimination as bad as the old ones." – as quoted in *Ronald Reagan: An American Life*.

- "Families stand at the center of our society. And every family has a personal stake in promoting excellence in education." – from the 1984 State of the Union Address.

- "Among the things he passed on to me were the belief that all men and women, regardless of their color or religion, are created equal and that individuals determine their own destiny; that is, it's largely their own ambition and hard work that determine their fate in life." – on the values instilled in him by his father as a child in Illinois, as quoted in *Ronald Reagan: An American Life*.

- "We do more for the under developed nations than anyone in the world but they act as if we're out to destroy them and they never say boo to the Soviets." – as quoted in *The Reagan Diaries*.

- "The frustrating thing is that those who are attacking religion claim they are doing it in the name of tolerance, freedom and open-mindedness. Question: Isn't the real truth that they are intolerant of religion? They refuse to tolerate its importance in our lives."

CHAPTER 15

THE ENEMY OF MY ENEMY IS MY FRIEND

The roles Ronald Reagan played in his film and television career were pretty straightforward and you could say, one dimensional. The good guys and bad guys were pretty clearly defined and in the end, the good guy always saved the day and got the girl. Those roles were reflective of American society through the 1950s—it was generally clear to Americans where the right and wrong sides of the line were.

But then along came the moral ambiguity of the 1960s.

The 1960s truly changed the way people saw and did things not just in America, but throughout the Western world. The Cold War may have seemed like a "black and white" event, but it was actually very complex and it wasn't always clear who the bad guys and good guys were.

Given his background, it wasn't always easy for Reagan to thrive in this type of environment. Reagan was a man who said that the Cold War was about "good and evil, right and wrong," so when he fought for the interests of his country, sometimes he had to make a deal with the devil. There is an ancient saying that is often translated as "the enemy of my enemy is my friend." Well, this proverb couldn't be more aptly applied than to Ronald Reagan's complex relationship with the Islamic extremist guerilla force known as the Mujahedeen in the 1980s.

Ronnie Makes Some Unlikely Friends

The term "mujahedeen" generally refers to any Islamic fundamentalist group that wages *jihad*, or religious war, against non-believers. Any number of groups throughout history, from all sects of Islam, can be defined as mujahedeen, but it was the Islamists who fought the Soviet Union in the 1980s who are generally known as *the* Mujahedeen.

The Afghan Mujahedeen formed after the Soviet Union invaded Afghanistan in 1979 to support the faltering Marxist government, leading to the start of the Soviet-Afghan War (1979-1989). Much as the Taliban has done in recent years with the American occupation of Afghanistan, the Mujahedeen specialized in ambush and other guerilla tactics to make the Soviet occupation of their country too costly to continue.

When Reagan assumed the presidency in 1981, he saw the war in Afghanistan as a potential way to forward his anti-communist agenda. Reagan quickly found out that the war in Afghanistan wasn't as cut and dry as many would believe. The Mujahedeen was comprised of Islamic extremists from around the world, including Osama Bin Laden, who hated the West and the US just as much as the Soviet Union. On the other hand, young Russian men were being killed in very brutal ways that reminded Reagan of what Americans had suffered through in Vietnam just ten years prior.

In addition to the hostile and some would say, unsavory background of the Mujahedeen, most Americans couldn't locate Afghanistan on a map. To be fair to Americans, though, most people in the world probably couldn't tell you where Afghanistan was. So, because the US is a democracy, Reagan had to sell the idea of giving financial and military support to a fundamentalist Islamic group to the American public and a Democrat-controlled House of Representatives.

Once again, Reagan employed his badass speaking and persuasion abilities to convince the American public that fighting a proxy war against the Soviet Union on the other side of the world was the right thing to do, and more importantly, he used some veteran political maneuvering to get enough Democrat support for the scheme.

Reagan even invited leaders of the Mujahedeen to the White House in 1983.

The combination of political bargaining and Reagan's persuasive abilities eventually got the Mujahedeen some arms and financial support from the US government, which was funneled to them by the CIA.

Quotes on War and the Military

- "There is first the threat of global war. No President, no Congress, no Prime Minister, no Parliament can spend a day entirely free of this threat. And I don't have to tell you that in today's world the existence of nuclear weapons could mean, if not the extinction of mankind, then surely the end of civilization as we know it. That's why negotiations on intermediate-range nuclear forces now underway in Europe and the START talks –Strategic Arms Reduction Talks – which will begin later this month, are not just critical to American or Western policy; they are critical to mankind." – from Ronald Reagan's "Ash Heap of History" speech on June 8, 1982.

- "Today, the United States stands as a beacon of liberty and democratic strength before the community of nations. We are resolved to stand firm against those who would destroy the freedoms we cherish. We are determined to achieve an enduring peace—a peace with liberty and with honor. This determination, this resolve, is the highest tribute we can pay to the many who have fallen in the service of our Nation." – Memorial Day speech on May 25, 1981.

- "There probably isn't any undertaking on earth short of assuring the national security that can't be handled more efficiently by the forces of private enterprise than by the federal government." – as quoted in *Ronald Reagan: An American Life*.

- "[I told the general] 'I think there ought to be a regulation that the president could return a salute inasmuch as he is commander in chief and civilian clothes are his uniform.' 'Well, if you did return a salute,' the general said, 'I don't think anyone would say anything to you about it.' The next time I got a salute, I saluted back. A big grin came over the marine's face, and down came his hand. From then on, I always returned salutes. When George Bush followed me into the White House, I encouraged him to keep up the tradition." – as quoted in *Ronald Reagan: An American Life*.

- "Our goal is peace. We can gain that peace by strengthening our alliances, by speaking candidly about the dangers before us, by assuring potential adversaries of our seriousness, by actively pursuing every chance of honest and fruitful negotiation." – Memorial Day speech at Arlington National Cemetery on May 31, 1982.

CHAPTER 16

EVEN BADASSES NEED FRIENDS

At times it seemed as though it was Reagan against most of the world. Sure, he had his wife and the majority of the American people on his side, but the media, much of the Democrat Party, and even a share of the Republican Party would have liked nothing more than to have seen Reagan run out of office in 1984 or, at the very least, have his power reduced by the Congress.

Not all American politicians shared Reagan's Cold War ideas of the world, and those who did were sometimes reticent to state them for fear of not being popular or as being seen as a "cowboy" like Reagan.

Over the years of his presidency, though, Reagan eventually developed some pretty close allies and friends around the world, with perhaps the most important and well-known being British Prime Minister Margaret Thatcher. In many ways, you can't talk about Reagan without discussing Thatcher. Thatcher's firm support for Reagan's foreign policies played a major role in American success, particularly in helping win the Cold War.

Margaret Thatcher was born Margaret Hilda Roberts on October 13, 1925, in Grantham, England to a middle-class family. As a young person, Margaret's parents always supported her interests, especially in academics, in which she excelled. Margaret's professional and personal life took off in the early 1950s: she married her life-long husband, David Thatcher in 1951; she became a barrister in 1953; and in 1959, Thatcher made the big step by entering Parliament as a minister from the Conservative Party.

And make no mistake about it; just because Thatcher was an empowered, strong woman, she wasn't a political liberal or a feminist. Well, not a feminist politically, although she never let attitudes toward women hold her back. Thatcher made quite a name for herself during the 1960s and did so despite being a woman in the most traditional, conservative political party in Britain at the time. After all, it wasn't called the "Conservative Party" for no reason.

But to understand Margaret Thatcher and her relationship with Ronald Reagan, you have to understand that she was a pragmatist above all. When she was once asked what the chances of Britain having a female prime minister, she gave this answer:

> "There will not be a woman prime minister in my lifetime – the male population is too prejudiced."

Just a few short years after making that statement, Thatcher would prove herself wrong.

The Iron Lady

Thatcher's rise through the jungle of British politics generally and the Conservative Party, in particular, was meteoric, to say the least. Thatcher's calm demeanor, articulate speech, and charm were an easy sell to the British people. She became the leader of the Conservatives in 1975, which was the opposition party at the time, and was then elevated to Prime Minister of the United Kingdom when the Conservative Party swept into power in 1979.

Britain had its first female prime minister and Ronald Reagan would have his staunchest ally and political confidant when he came into power.

Margaret Thatcher was every bit the anti-communist that Ronald Reagan was and was also not afraid to mix it up with her domestic political enemies, whether they were in the opposition Labour Party, the media, the Irish Republican Army (IRA), or the powerful unions. Thatcher's domestic policies, which became known as "Thatcherism," also followed a very Reaganesque economic platform that included deregulation, lower taxes, and opposition to the labor unions.

In terms of the British military, Thatcher led an increase in overall spending on more financial and troop commitments to NATO, which angered the Labor Party and many on Britain's left but was music to Reagan's ears. In Reagan's two terms as president, Anglo-American relations were at a level not seen since World War II. It was clear that the leaders of the two countries shared not only political beliefs but a genuine friendship that seemed to bring a new sense of unity to the English-speaking world.

Thatcher's generally tough exterior and militantly anti-communist views earned her the nickname the "Iron Lady" from a Soviet journalist in 1976. Perhaps it was meant as an insult, but in true badass fashion, Thatcher turned it around to be a symbol of her strength.

REAGAN QUOTES ABOUT THATCHER AND THATCHER QUOTES ABOUT REAGAN

- "Ronald Reagan knew his own mind. He had firm principles - and, I believe, the right ones. He expounded them clearly, he acted upon them decisively." – Margaret Thatcher in her eulogy to Ronald Reagan in 2004.

- "As I prepare to depart this office in January, I take considerable satisfaction in knowing that Margaret Thatcher will still reside at Number Ten, Downing Street, and will be there to offer President Bush her friendship, cooperation and advice." – public statement just before he left office.

- "We share laws and literature, blood, and moral fiber." – statement to the press after he met with Thatcher for the first time at the White House in 1981.

- "She is the best man in England." – 1983 statement to the press about Margaret Thatcher.

- "The second most important man in my life." – Margaret Thatcher on her political and personal relationship with Ronald Reagan.

CHAPTER 17

BRINGING THE COLD WAR TO SPACE

If you grew up in the United States during the 1980s, then you probably remember the general feeling that the Soviet Union could attack at any time. Of course, movies like *Red Dawn* and *The Day After* did their fair share to scare the average American into believing that the Russians were just around the corner waiting to invade by stealth. Or perhaps that a situation of miscommunication and overzealous generals on either side could lead to World War III.

But on the other hand, it was the decade of excess, where the economy was very strong by the middle of the decade and capitalism was far from the dirty word it is today in many quarters.

So, to put it mildly, the 1980s was a bit of a strange time and so it took a somewhat unconventional leader to bring the United States through it. Ronnie was going to make sure that the American economy kept chugging along, producing more and more millionaires, and the only way to do that was by keeping the communists at bay. We've already seen how Reagan took a tough line on communism by supporting the

Mujahedeen and generally not caring what his opponents thought, but in 1983, he took the struggle to a whole new level by introducing "Star Wars."

The Real-Life Star Wars

We've seen that a large part of why Reagan was such an effective politician, and a badass, was because he knew the importance of public image and how to effectively use it for his advantage. After all, Reagan was a former Hollywood actor who was one of the best public-speaking presidents of all time, so when he rolled out his idea to protect the United States through an intercontinental ballistic missile defense system known as the Strategic Defense Initiative (SDI) people listened.

The American and the Soviet philosophy in regard to their nuclear arsenals at that point was Mutually Assured Destruction (MAD), which as the name denotes, was a "strategy" whereby either side hoped the other wouldn't strike first because to do so would only mean destruction for everyone. Not much of a strategy, was it?

Well, Reagan also didn't think it was a very good strategy, so when he took the oath of the presidency, he quickly brought together America's greatest scientists, physicists, and engineers to develop SDI, and on March 232, 1983, he addressed the nation in a televised speech about the program, stating:

> "I call upon the scientific community who gave us nuclear weapons to turn their great talents to the cause of

mankind and world peace: to give us the means of rendering these nuclear weapons impotent and obsolete."

The reaction to the speech was immediate and intense.

The Soviet leaders showed their disapproval; apparently they thought that everyone would just be fine with pointing guns at each other perpetually. Reagan's Democrat and media critics also jumped on the SDI proposal, stating that it would harm any diplomatic progress made with the Russians and that it could trigger a war instead of preventing one. One of Reagan's biggest political opponents, liberal Massachusetts Senator Ted Kennedy, even referred to the SDI as "reckless Star Wars schemes" to the *Washington Post.*

And so the famous term was born!

Just like every other potential obstacle in Reagan's career, he took the lampooning of SDI by his political enemies and used it to his advantage. In his matter-of-fact style of speech, Reagan explained to the American people why he believed SDI was important, and despite its complexity, some of how it worked. Reagan also knew that, no matter how much his critics made fun of SDI by calling it Star Wars, it wouldn't hurt its perception.

The third *Star Wars* movie was about to come out when Reagan delivered his speech, so if anything, most people thought it was cool to nickname SDI "Star Wars."

Behind the scenes, Reagan knew that he'd never see SDI completed. Some of the space-based weapons were just too complex for the time, and many still are, but like a true badass, he was playing the long game. Reagan knew that the

SDI program would force the Soviets to keep parity with the Americans in defense budget spending. That meant, between the Afghan War and its expensive nuclear arsenal, the Soviet Union was getting closer and closer to bankruptcy.

Ronnie knew that if the United States was going to defeat the Soviet Union and win the Cold War cleanly, it would be done through the dollar, not the gun.

QUOTES ABOUT FREEDOM

- "Freedom is never more than one generation away from extinction. We didn't pass it to our children in the bloodstream. It must be fought for, protected, and handed on for them to do the same, or one day we will spend our sunset years telling our children and our children's children what it was once like in the United States where men were free."

- "I hope we once again have reminded people that man is not free unless government is limited. There's a clear cause and effect here that is as neat and predictable as a law of physics: As government expands, liberty contracts."

- "Freedom prospers when religion is vibrant and the rule of law under God is acknowledged."

- "We will always remember. We will always be proud. We will always be prepared, so we will always be free."

- "Our natural, inalienable rights are now considered to be a dispensation from government, and freedom has never been so fragile, so close to slipping from our grasp as it is at this moment."

CHAPTER 18

VOODOO ECONOMICS?

When Reagan assumed office in 1981, he faced many problems. The Cold War and his war against communism seemed to encapsulate and symbolize most of his presidency, but the most pressing matter he had to face was the economy. You've no doubt heard the term "it's the economy, stupid" at least once in your life, and when it comes to politics, it's certainly true.

Reagan could never have supported the Mujahedeen, initiated Star Wars, or supported any of his numerous other anti-communist programs if he didn't do something about the economy. And in 1981, to say the American economy was a hot mess was an understatement.

The 1970s was one long decade that most people would like to forget. The clothing styles sucked, the music was cheesy, and the economy was among the worst in American history. Thanks to a little foresight and social safety nets, the economy wasn't as bad as it had been during the Great Depression, but it wasn't a whole lot better. There was a constant feeling of dread among Americans in the 1970s that the bottom could fall out of the economy at any moment, but instead, it just limped along with high inflation, above-average unemployment, and by the end of the decade, a fuel crisis.

Americans elected Reagan to take care of all those problems. Sure, his stance against communism and other social issues made many people like him, but it was his clear, well-articulated economic ideas that were the meat behind the issues that got him elected.

Reaganomics

When Reagan was inaugurated in 1981, he faced a slew of economic problems: the unemployment rate was over 7%, gas cost $1.31 a gallon (I know, I know, but remember this was 40 years ago!), and the inflation rate was near a whopping 9%. Every politician and economist knew that something had to be done; the bottom might not drop out of the economy, but keeping it as is in a constant state of "stagflation" — as it became known — was also unacceptable.

So, when Reagan was running for office, he outlined his plan, which included across the board decreases in government spending, deregulation of laws and policies toward certain industries, lowering taxes, and reducing the money supply. All of this may seem like standard Republican economic policies today and were, for the most part, even followed by Democrat President Bill Clinton, but in the late 1970s and early '80s, these ideas were controversial. Since the Great Depression, American politicians of both parties generally followed Keynesian economic policies, which — without getting too deep into economics — generally involves heavy government spending to keep unemployment low. Many

Republicans scoffed at Reagan's ideas. George H.W. Bush, who would later become Reagan's vice president, called Reagan's ideas "voodoo economics" because he said it involved a lot of magic and misdirection.

Essentially, it was a simple economic theory that was based on supply-side economics. Reagan argued that, once the interest rates and taxes were lowered, the wealthy would invest more in the economy, which in turn would "trickle down" to the middle class, earning it the nickname "trickle-down economics" among many economists.

Despite general misgivings within the Republic Party, Ronnie was able to convince the Republican-controlled Senate to go along with his economic policy, which became known as "Reaganomics" to those who favored it and "voodoo economics" to its critics.

Getting the Democrat-controlled House on board was another matter.

Ronnie used executive orders and presidential control over certain parts of the economy to enact some of his changes, while he used his badass oratorical and compromising skills to get the Democrats to go along with parts of his economic plan, such as taxes, that needed to go through Congress.

By 1983, the economy was taking off, with unemployment dropping significantly, inflation going down, the GDP significantly increasing, and a new sense of economic optimism.

Quotes on Economics

- "I've never been able to understand why a Republican contributor is a 'fat cat' and a Democratic contributor of the same amount of money is a 'public-spirited philanthropist'."

- "We don't have a trillion-dollar debt because we haven't taxed enough; we have a trillion-dollar debt because we spend too much."

- "Government's view of the economy could be summed up in a few short phrases: If it moves, tax it. If it keeps moving, regulate it. And if it stops moving, subsidize it."

- "Recession is when your neighbor loses his job. Depression is when you lose yours. And recovery is when Jimmy Carter loses his."

- "The best minds are not in government. If any were, business would steal them away."

CHAPTER 19

GRENADA, MEET RONNIE

If you had have asked most Americans in 1983 — or today, and really, just about any nationality in the world in addition to Americans — to find "Grenada" on a map, most probably couldn't. A few may have pointed to the town or county in Mississippi or maybe the more worldly would point to the city of *Granada* in Spain, but most would have had no idea where the actual country of Grenada was. And honestly, you can't blame them. In case you don't know, and let's face it, you probably don't, Grenada is a small Caribbean island nation of just over 100,000 people. Today, it is best known as being an exporter of nutmeg and a minor tourist location, but in 1983, it became the scene of a Cold War battle.

It was a battle Ronnie didn't intend to lose. Reagan got to show America and the world once more what a badass he was when he decided to invade Grenada, despite cries of protest from the United Nations and even the United Kingdom.

Reagan's ordered invasion of Grenada was so badass that it even spawned the badass military movie, *Heartbreak Ridge*, starring legendary silver screen badass Clint Eastwood.

Communism in America's Backyard

When Fidel Castro took over Cuba in 1959, the Western hemisphere got its first socialist/communist nation. Things took off pretty quickly after that, with the attempted Bay of Pigs Invasion, the Cuban Missile Crisis, and at least a couple of attempted assassination attempts by members of organized crime, Cuban exiles, and the CIA. As a result of the Cuban Missile Crisis, the US agreed to leave Cuba alone, but that wasn't a promise to not actively fight to keep communism out of the rest of the Americas.

Throughout the 1970s, the US government supported various right-wing dictatorships and military juntas throughout Latin America and the Caribbean—if they were dedicated anti-communists. When Carter was president, though, the support for those governments eased a bit and leftist guerilla groups gained ground and a Marxist government even came to power in Nicaragua in 1979 (we'll get to Ronnie's reaction to that a bit later). Among the countries of the Americas "turning red" at this time was the otherwise inconsequential former British colony of Grenada.

In 1974 the United Kingdom gave Grenada its independence, but as often is the case in that part of the world, political violence quickly followed. An armed revolution, supported by Cuba, brought a communist government into power in 1979. None of this was welcome news for the American government, but due to the country's small size, it was relatively tolerated. Even when Ronnie became president, Grenada was far down on his list of countries to deal with.

But then things got out of hand in 1983.

Socialist Grenada was led by Maurice Bishop from 1979 until October 16, 1983. Although Bishop was a true red Marxist, he was also a pragmatist. He knew that his tiny island nation needed to keep Western tourist money flowing in and that cutting off all relations with the United States and other capitalist countries could lead to ruin. Because of this attitude, Deputy Prime Minister Bernard Coard led a coup on October 16, 1983 and had Bishop arrested for not being communist enough. He later had him executed.

Reagan knew that something probably had to be done in Grenada. The situation was made even more complicated by the fact that there was a considerable number of Cuban military and civilian advisors in the country on the one hand, and on the other, there were a lot of American medical school students on the island.

The US invasion of Grenada began on the morning of October 25, 1983, and it was over before it began.

The American forces numbered over 7,000 as opposed to the more than 1,000 Grenadians and nearly 1,000 Cuban advisors. But it wasn't just the numbers. The Americans had ships, planes, and tanks, while Grenada had none. The Americans sent in their top units — Rangers, Airborne, and Marine Recon — to quickly and efficiently take control. Only 19 Americans were killed, Coard was arrested, and Grenada's government took a much more friendly tone toward the US.

The reaction to the invasion was mixed. In addition to the UN's opposition, the Soviet Union was obviously against it, but perhaps somewhat surprisingly, so was the United Kingdom.

In the end, though, it didn't matter what these other countries thought because a true badass is always willing to go against the grain and walk alone. But Ronnie didn't have to walk totally alone, as the American public supported the invasion.

The Invasion of Grenada may not have amounted to very much, but it played an important role in the construction of the image of Ronald Reagan as a rough and tough, badass president. Reagan wasn't afraid to use force, even if it wasn't popular, and he also knew that a quick military victory over a small foe such as Grenada would help Americans get over the loss of Vietnam.

As Reagan said shortly after the Grenada Invasion:

> "Our days of weakness are over. Our military forces are back on their feet and standing tall."

Quotes about Work

- "There is no limit to the amount of good you can do if you don't care who gets the credit."

- "I've heard that hard work never killed anyone, but I say why take the chance?"

- "Entrepreneurs and their small enterprises are responsible for almost all the economic growth in the United States."

- "Welfare's purpose should be to eliminate, as far as possible, the need for its own existence."

- "I learned that hard work is an essential part of life—that by and large, you don't get something for nothing—and that America was a place that offered unlimited opportunity to those who did work hard. I learned to admire risk takers and entrepreneurs, be they farmers or small merchants, who went to work and took risks to build something for themselves and their children, pushing at the boundaries of their lives to make them better. I have always wondered at this American marvel, the great energy of the human soul that drives people to better themselves and improve the fortunes of their families and communities. Indeed, I know of no greater force on earth." – as quoted in *Ronald Reagan: An American Life*.

CHAPTER 20

NOT TOO PROUD
TO ADMIT DEFEAT

A defining characteristic of any good leader, and most badasses, is the ability to admit when you've lost, or at least admit when it's time for a "strategic retreat." Badass leaders continually show bravery in the face of danger, but they never rush headlong into battles—both figuratively and literally—that could cost them valuable resources. The ancient Greek king Pyrrhus may have been brave, but he was also known to be reckless and foolhardy, which is how the term "Pyrrhic Victory" began. No, a true badass is also a good leader who always knows when to say enough is enough.

Just two days before Reagan ordered the invasion of Grenada, he was faced with an incredible decision in the Middle East. It was one that could have cost him his presidency and it certainly made some war hawks question his decision making, but it also probably saved many American lives.

This was the October 23, 1983 bombing of the joint US-French military barracks in Beirut, Lebanon. The bombing left 241 American Marines and 58 French soldier's dead, sending a wave of anger throughout the United States.

Reagan's reaction, though, showed that sometimes there's more to a badass than a tough exterior.

Before Al-Qaeda

For many Americans, contact and knowledge of the Islamic world generally and the Middle East, in particular, began after the terrorist attacks of September 11, 2001. It was certainly a tragic event that changed the way Americans looked at the world, and the way the world looked at Americans and the United States. However the US already had a long and complicated relationship with the Middle East before those attacks.

As we've already discussed in an earlier chapter, the Islamic Revolution in Iran certainly put a dampener on Persian-American relations, to say the least. Yet numerous hot spots flared up throughout the Middle East in the 1970s and '80s and the United States slowly but surely became involved.

The US's steadfast support for Israel put it at odds with Syria and Egypt for a time and when the Lebanese Civil War (1975-1991) broke out, it threatened to destabilize the region and possibly the world.

Before 1975, Lebanon was among the most peaceful and prosperous of all the countries in the region and at the time had a slight majority Christian population. That background made it a bridge between West and East throughout history, but by the mid-1970s, sectarian differences, the Cold War, and the growth of radical Islam had ripped the country apart.

The Lebanese Civil War was extremely confusing and destructive. The Christian-dominated government was supported by Christian militias and the government of Israel, to a certain extent. Radical Sunni Muslims and Palestinian refugees, who fought under the umbrella of the Palestine Liberation Organization (PLO) opposed the government and Christian forces and sometimes allied with each other. Shia Muslim militant groups, such as Hezbollah, also opposed the government and were supported by the Syrian government. But the Shias and Syria also opposed Israel and the Sunni militants.

There were also communists and leftist militias who received support from the Soviet Union and other communist states.

Needless to say, it was a complete cluster****.

Reagan got involved in the situation when he brokered a ceasefire between Israel and the PLO in 1981, which then led to the creation of the Multinational Force in Lebanon (MNF). The force was comprised of American, British, Italian, and French military units with the intent of keeping the multitude of militant factions in Lebanon away from each other.

Needless to say, the fighting continued and to the Shia, Sunni, and Druze factions, it appeared as though the MNF was supporting the Christian militias. So, on October 23, 1983, a suicide bomber drove a truck bomb into the US Marine barracks and minutes later, another did the same at the French barracks. The Shia group Islamic Jihad claimed responsibility for the attacks, stating that they wanted all Western powers out of Lebanon.

In addition to the Marines killed, more than 100 were wounded, making it the worst single-day toll for the Marines since the Battle of Iwo Jima in 1945.

Reagan was in quite a predicament. The situation in Grenada was taking place at the same time; theoretically, he could have ordered an attack on both countries, but the situation in Lebanon was so messy. In modern civil wars, the armies are rarely clearly marked, and Lebanon just didn't seem important enough to risk more American lives. Although plenty of war hawks were whispering in Ronnie's ears to unleash the dogs of war on Lebanon, he declined and instead decided to pull all the troops out from the country.

Instead of hurting Reagan politically, ordering the pullout only seemed to help him in the polls. He showed that, as tough as he could be, he wasn't reckless and that he did care about American lives. American military personnel were not just cannon fodder for Ronnie.

Besides, he would later have other chances in the Middle East.

QUOTES ABOUT PATRIOTISM

- "America is a shining city upon a hill whose beacon light guides freedom-loving people everywhere." – in his 1989 Farewell Address to the Nation.

- "The United States had a constitution, I said, that was different from all the others because in it the people tell their government what it can do." – as quoted in *Ronald Reagan: An American Life.*

- "Yes, our country has its shortcomings, but there's no moral equivalency between democracy and totalitarianism... There's no moral equivalency between propaganda and the truth."

- "The American dream is not that every man must be level with every other man. The American dream is that every man must be free to become whatever God intends he should become."

- "We were taught, very directly, what it means to be an American. And we absorbed, almost in the air, a love of country and an appreciation of its institutions. If you didn't get these things from your family you got them from the neighborhood... Or you could get a sense of patriotism from school. And if all else failed you could get a sense of patriotism from the popular culture." – in his 1989 Farewell Address to the Nation.

CHAPTER 21

NOT SINCE FDR

By the time the 1984 election campaign season got underway, it would be an understatement to say that momentum was going Reagan's way. The president's economic policies seemed to be working, as the recession and stagflation had given way to an economic boom, and globally American power was once again respected and had become a source of pride for Americans. Because of this, there was only minimal opposition to Reagan during the presidential primaries and he easily won re-nomination.

The situation with the Democrats, though, was a little more complicated.

Because the Democrats faced such a monumental challenge, they believed they had to pick a candidate more to the left to distance themselves as much as possible from Reagan. They thought that, by doing so, they could paint a contrast with the president and hopefully energize the left-wing base of their party. The Democrat primaries were toughly contested and featured a loaded field of candidates, but by the time the party held its convention, the two remaining candidates were black activist Jesse Jackson and former Minnesota senator and vice president under Jimmy Carter, Walter Mondale.

The delegates ultimately picked Mondale, believing that Jackson was too radical and that, if anyone could pull off a miracle, it would be a farm boy from the Midwest.

But what makes a miracle become a miracle, is because they seldom happen.

A Badass Will Not Be Denied

Mondale knew he had a herculean task in front of him, so he decided to make news by picking New York congresswoman Geraldine Ferraro as his running mate. The move was done to help shore up the women's vote, possibly win New York, and just to steal some of the thunder from the Reagan campaign.

But a true badass like Reagan can never be denied.

Although Reagan consistently polled far ahead of Mondale, the president didn't rest on his laurels and hit the campaign trail. Mondale ran on an anti-nuclear, pro-tax, and pro-Equal Rights Amendment campaign, while Reagan decided to focus his campaign on the accomplishments from his first term.

The Reagan campaign eventually centered around the "Morning in America" concept, which was the name of one of his ads and later became the de facto slogan of the campaign. The narration of the ad read:

> "It's morning again in America. Today more men and women will go to work than ever before in our country's history. With interest rates at about half the record highs of 1980, nearly 2,000 families today will buy new homes, more than at any time in the past four years. This afternoon 6,500 young men and women will be married,

91

and with inflation at less than half of what it was just four years ago, they can look forward with confidence to the future. It's morning again in America, and under the leadership of President Reagan, our country is prouder and stronger and better. Why would we ever want to return to where we were less than four short years ago?"

For most Americans in 1984, the answer was clear: No, they didn't want to return to the awful 1970s.

Reagan and Mondale both campaign tirelessly around the country, but the true highlights of the 1984 presidential campaign were the two debates between the candidates on October 7 and October 21, with more than 60 million people watching each. Although Mondale held his own and remained quite composed, he was no match for the Great Communicator.

The big turning point, though, came during the October 21 debate in Kansas City, Missouri. After Reagan made a few gaffs and seemed a bit off in the first debate, the moderator of the second debate asked the president if age was a legitimate issue. The great communicator's response was perhaps the most memorable quote of any American presidential debate:

> "I will not make age an issue of this campaign. I am not going to exploit, for political purposes, my opponent's youth and inexperience."

Even Mondale had to laugh at the response, but the quip ensured Ronnie would win a second term as president.

On election night on November 6, there wasn't much debate over *if* Reagan would win, it was more a matter of by how much. Once the results were finally counted, it went down as one of the greatest presidential landslides in American history. Reagan won 525 electoral votes to Mondale's 13. Mondale only won his home state of Minnesota, just barely, and the reliably Democrat District of Columbia. It was the most one-sided electoral victory since President Franklin Delano Roosevelt defeated Alf Landon (who?) in the 1936 election. In terms of the popular vote, which doesn't matter in the US presidential election, Reagan won nearly 17 million more votes than Mondale, which was second only to President Richard Nixon's popular vote victory margin over George McGovern (who?) in 1972.

No doubt about it, Reagan's 1984 was completely badass, setting the tone for some interesting and important things that happened in his second term.

QUOTES ABOUT CULTURE

- "A nation that cannot control its borders is not a nation."

- "Our government needs the church, because only those humble enough to admit they're sinners can bring democracy the tolerance it requires to survive."

- "Let me speak plainly: The United States of America is and must remain a nation of openness to people of all beliefs. Our very unity has been strengthened by this pluralism. That's how we began; this is how we must always be. The ideals of our country leave no room whatsoever for intolerance, anti-Semitism, or bigotry of any kind—none. The unique thing about America is a wall in our Constitution separating church and state. It guarantees there will never be a state religion in this land, but at the same time it makes sure that every single American is free to choose and practice his or her religious beliefs or to choose no religion at all. Their rights shall not be questioned or violated by the state." - speech at the International Convention of the B'nai B'rith organization on September 6, 1984.

- "I occasionally think how quickly our differences worldwide would vanish if we were facing an alien threat from outside this world."

- "My parents constantly drummed into me the importance of judging people as individuals. There was no more grievous sin at our household than a racial slur or other evidence of religious or racial intolerance. A lot of it, I think, was because my dad had learned what discrimination was like firsthand. He'd grown up in an era when some stores still had signs at their door saying, NO DOGS OR IRISHMEN ALLOWED." – as quoted in *Ronald Reagan: An American Life*

CHAPTER 22

THE BADASS PRESIDENT AND THE BADASS POPE

Next to Margaret Thatcher, Pope John Paul II was probably Reagan's biggest ally in terms of international affairs. The pope may not have commanded an army, but he did have the ear of the largest community of Christians in the world, with more than one billion followers. And despite their very different backgrounds, John Paul II and Ronald Reagan had more than few things in common that brought them together.

Like Reagan, John Paul II survived an assassin's bullet after he was shot on May 13, 1981, just two months after the president was shot. The would-be assassin, Mehmet Ali Ağca of Turkey, was determined to be a crazed lone wolf, but rumors persisted, and still do, that the KGB was behind the hit. Although there's no proof that the Soviet Union tried to have the pope killed, there is little doubt that they viewed him as a thorn in their side, to say the least. Pope John Paul II, who was born Karol Józef Wojtyła in Poland in 1920, was an outspoken anti-communist, just like Reagan.

Solidarity

Although Poland was a member of the communist military alliance, the Warsaw Pact, it was a reluctant member at best. Most Poles never really bought into the idea of communism, so when the Americans and other Western powers began looking for a way to tear down the Iron Curtain, they often looked at Poland as the key.

When Pope John Paul I died in 1978 after serving in the office for just 33 days, Wojtyła was elected to the highest office in the Church, becoming John Paul II. It became very clear early on that John Paul II wasn't going to be just another pope who lived high on the hog off the Vatican's coffers. No, John Paul II was going to use his office to make a difference.

In 1980, the Solidarity movement formed in John Paul II's home country of Poland. The Solidarity movement was a union of dockworkers in Gdansk, but only unions sanctioned by the communist governments were considered legal, so the workers were breaking the law every time they held a demonstration or protest.

Despite many Solidarity workers being beaten and/or imprisoned and the government declaring martial law, the movement continued to grow. A large part of the reason why Solidarity grew was that John Paul II spoke in its favor when he traveled the world and so too did Reagan when he spoke to the American people.

Although Ronnie was raised a Protestant, he had a deep respect for all religious faiths, especially Christian ones. Reagan was determined to win the Cold War and he knew that the only way he could do that was by getting international support. He had already gained Thatcher's steadfast support, which was good militarily, but Reagan knew that the Cold War was probably not going to be won on an actual battlefield; it would be won in people's hearts and minds.

So, he needed to find a spiritual ally in the war against communism.

Not long after he was elected president in 1981, Reagan began corresponding with John Paul II, but curiously, the United States did not officially recognize the Vatican as a sovereign state until January 10, 1984. Once the US recognized the Vatican, Reagan's support for John Paul II's anti-communist crusade, particularly in Poland, became crucial.

The two leaders met several times throughout the 1980s, and together with Thatcher, they formed a sort of badass anti-communist triumvirate that ultimately won the Cold War. Reagan was the cowboy leading the charge, John Paul II was the priest blessing the troops as they headed into battle, and Thatcher put a feminine, softer touch on it all.

There was no way the Soviet Union could have defeated that alliance!

Miscellaneous Quotes

- "A president should never say never. But I'm going to violate that rule and say never. I will never stand for a reduction in the social security benefits for the people now getting them." – at the October 7, 1984 presidential debate against Walter Mondale.

- "Just because I've come from London I have the this urge to quote the great Dr. Johnson who said, 'the feeling for friendship is like that of being comfortably filled with roast beef.' Well I feel very much filled with friendship this afternoon and I bring you the warmest regards and goodwill of the American people." –from the June 9, 1982 address to the Bundestag in Bonn, West Germany.

- "America you are beautiful . . . and blessed . . . . The ultimate test of your greatness is the way you treat every human being, but especially the weakest and most defenseless. If you want equal justice for all and true freedom and lasting peace, then America, defend life." – Pope John Paul II, as quoted in *A Pilgrim Pope: Messages for the World.*

- "The future doesn't belong to the light-hearted. It belongs to the brave."

- "Surround yourself with great people; delegate authority; get out of the way."

CHAPTER 23

SO BADASS HE HAD A DOCTRINE NAMED AFTER HIM

We've seen that Ronald Reagan was pretty much born a badass, so by the time he became the president, he knew how to handle himself in tricky situations. He had to overcome a weak economy domestically, but it was in the realm of foreign affairs where he truly earned his reputation as a badass. That is where all American presidents have established their badass bona fides.

You could say it all began with the fifth American president, James Monroe. When Monroe was in power from 1817 to 1828, plenty of change was happening in the Western Hemisphere. Most of the colonies of Spain and Portugal in Latin American declared and earned their independence through revolutions during that time. Although most Americans generally had little to do with events south of the border, they were mostly supportive of the liberation movements and were glad to see the European colonial powers out of the Americas.

President Monroe let it be known, in no uncertain terms, that any attempts by the European powers to recolonize the Americas would be met by American arms. Monroe's policy became known as the "Monroe Doctrine."

In the 150 plus years after, the term "doctrine" was occasionally used after a president's name to describe their foreign policy philosophy. Very few presidents have a doctrine named after them, though, which indicates a certain level of badassness for those that do.

President Harry Truman announced his doctrine to the Congress in 1947 as one that would actively contain the spread of communism around the globe. Likewise, his successor Dwight Eisenhower announced a doctrine that specifically sought to limit the influence of the Soviet Union in the Middle East.

But the most aggressive and expansive of all presidential doctrines was the "Reagan Doctrine." By the time Reagan announced his doctrine in his State of the Union Address on February 6, 1985, he had already been carrying it out for several years. It was essentially not just to contain communism, but to aggressively fight it on every corner of the globe, using whatever means necessary in a policy that became known as "rollback."

The Reagan Doctrine was extremely controversial, and nearly landed Reagan in legal jeopardy, but it was what defined his presidency.

Better Dead Than Red

We've already seen how Ronald Reagan evolved from a standard liberal into a staunch conservative who made fighting communism the backbone of his life's philosophy. To Reagan, the values upon which the Founding Fathers built the American system the epitome of righteousness, so therefore, anything associated with communism and socialism was inherently evil.

As Reagan moved up the ladder of the American political and government system, he was able to apply his anti-communist thoughts more effectively and at the same time, refine them. Reagan opposed the leftist students at Berkeley while he was governor of California and by the time he became president, he was able to apply that philosophy more widely.

Supporting the Mujahedeen and various right-wing insurgency groups in communist nations, and right-wing and military dictatorships in other nations (we'll get to that in a minute), was the primary way in which Reagan carried out his doctrine.

Thanks to the Reagan Doctrine, the United States was actively involved in "proxy wars" from Afghanistan to Angola, and from Nicaragua to points across the Middle East. If there was some type of war involving communism during the 1980s, you can be sure that Ronnie was getting involved.

Some of the individuals and groups he supported were unsavory, to say the least, and there was considerable pushback from the Democrat Party regarding funding, but the American people generally supported the Reagan Doctrine.

Ronnie used his speaking skills to assure the American people that supporting questionable leaders in countries they knew little about was vital to protect the American dream. Few people could have pulled off that task, but Reagan wasn't like most people, was he?

Quotes about Communism

- "The Sandinista revolution in Nicaragua turned out to be just an exchange of one set of autocratic rulers for another, and the people still had no freedom, no democratic rights, and more poverty." – August 27, 1983 speech to the US Congress about the spread of communism in Central America.

- "When Nikita Khrushchev has told his people he knows what our answer will be? He has told them that we are retreating under the pressure of the Cold War, and someday when the time comes to deliver the final ultimatum, our surrender will be voluntary because by that time we will have weakened from within spiritually, morally, and economically. He believes this because from our side he has heard voices pleading for peace at any price or better Red than dead, or as one commentator put it, he would rather live on his knees than die on his feet." – from the 1964 "Time for Choosing" speech.

- "A little less detente with the Politbureau and more encouragement to the dissenters might be worth a lot of armored divisions."

- "I don't believe any reasonable observer can deny that there is a threat to both peace and freedom today. It is as stark as that gash of a border that separates the German people. We're menaced by a power that openly condemns our values and answers our restraint with a relentless military buildup. We cannot simply assume every nation wants the peace we so earnestly desire." – June 9, 1982 address to the Bundestag in Bonn, West Germany.

- "We should not and we will not protect the Nicaraguan government from the anger of its own people." – August 27, 1983 speech to the US Congress about the spread of communism in Central America.

CHAPTER 24

DEALING WITH THE DEMOCRATS

For some of you reading this the 1980s may not seem very long ago, but in terms of politics, it's like a lifetime. Sure, the US government system is the same and the Republicans and Democrats are still the only true games in town, but the nature of the people those parties attract and how they deal with each other has drastically changed.

Unless you've had your head stuck in the sand, you'll know that politics in general has become a lot more divisive since the 1980s, which is no fault of Reagan's. When it came to political parties, Ronnie was willing to look past the labels and partisan divides to carry out his policies.

Reagan was also able to appeal to traditional Democrat voters in a way that no politician had done before in a America, all without sacrificing his ideals. And that ability to negotiate with the Democrats on certain policies without compromising his core principles is one more factor that made Reagan such an effective badass-in-chief.

Politics is a Dirty Game

Most people, regardless of their party affiliation, ethnic or national background, religion, or age will agree that, despite its sometimes obvious defects, democracy is the best political system. After all, if it was good enough for the Athenians 2,500 years ago, it must be good enough for us today, right?

Well, one of the problems of democracy, when compared to totalitarianism, is its seeming lack of efficiency. The government is controlled by different factions or parties that are competing with rival parties to either keep power or gain power. Because of this, things usually move slowly in democracies and there is sometimes a tendency by some to "play dirty."

When Ronnie became president in 1981, he was faced with a House of Representatives held by the Democrats, many of whom resented him personally and for his beliefs. As a former governor, Reagan was also a Washington "outsider," quickly learning that those who live inside the "Beltway" brought cunning, deceit, and "dirty politics" to a whole new level.

Despite these obstacles, Ronnie had a few things in his favor. The Senate was controlled by the Republicans, who steadfastly supported him, which meant that at worst, Congress would be in a stalemate. Then there was Reagan's ability to charm the people and his superb speaking skills as the Great Communicator, which allowed him to win over some Democratic members of Congress along with the American people.

But perhaps the most important part of Reagan's success in dealing with the Democrats in Congress was his ability sway the rank-and-file of the Democrat Party's base.

As a former Democrat himself, Reagan was able to talk to American Democrats in an understanding tone. The combination of his economic and foreign policy ideas appealed to Democrats in the "Rust Belt" states; so much so that he was able to build a new constituency group with them that became known as the "Reagan Democrats." The Reagan Democrats were primarily white, middle-income, and blue-collar workers, often union members, who saw themselves as social conservatives in a country that seemed to be marching quickly to the left after the 1960s.

There is no way Reagan would have won such lopsided victories without the Reagan Democrats and they were the group who ensured that the Democrats in Congress would work with the president.

Once Ronnie had the Reagan Democrats on board with his agenda, he was able to leverage their support when dealing with the congressional Democrats, taking a page from their political playbook. Reagan Democrats often "split tickets," voting for Democrats for Congress, governor, and in state and local elections, but supporting Reagan 100%. If Congress members went too hard against Reagan's agenda, he singled them out, so his Reagan Democrat supporters let their Democrat Party know that their support had limits.

By building ties with working-class Democrats, Ronald Reagan was able to effectively control the Democrat opposition during both terms of his presidency. Seasoned political operatives from all political parties will be the first to tell you that Ronnie's ability to do so was truly a badass political move.

Quotes about Politics

- "It isn't so much that liberals are ignorant. It's just that they know so many things that aren't so."

- "It has been said that politics is the second oldest profession. I have learned that it bears a striking resemblance to the first."

- "Every president since this country has assumed global responsibilities has known that those responsibilities could only be met if we pursued a bipartisan foreign policy." –

- August 27, 1983 speech to the US Congress about the spread of communism in Central America.

- "Any issue that comes before me I have instructed Cabinet members and staff, they are not to bring up any of the political ramifications that might surround the issue. I don't want to hear them. I want to hear only arguments as to whether it is good or bad for the people. Is it morally right. And on that basis and on that basis alone, we make a decision on every issue." – at the October 7, 1984 presidential debate against Walter Mondale.

- "I think growing up in a small town is a good foundation for anyone who decides to enter politics. You get to know people as individuals, not as blocs or members of special interest groups." – in *Ronald Reagan: An American Life*.

CHAPTER 25

GADDAFI MEETS HIS MATCH

Long before Osama Bin Laden was the man from the Middle East Americans loved to hate, there was Muammar Gaddafi. Gaddafi was the extremely eccentric (that's putting it mildly) dictator of the North African nation of Libya from 1969 until he was executed in a Western-sponsored coup in 2011. Although, like Bin Laden, Gaddafi was from the Middle East and nominally a Muslim, the two men fought for different causes.

Gaddafi's ideology drifted from Arab nationalism to Marxism and back again, with a tinge of Islamism mixed in from time to time. At no time during his rule of Libya did he ever support Salafist Muslims like Bin Laden or the Muslim Brotherhood; he often imprisoned or killed supporters of those ideas.

But Gaddafi was supported by the Soviet Union and he was truly a loose cannon, which put him right in the middle of Reagan's crosshairs.

To be honest, Reagan probably really didn't know what to make of Gaddafi. In 1981, the guy had been in power for more than ten years as dictator, yet never promoted himself past colonel. His public statements were strange, to say the least, and his style was even more unpredictable: one day he'd be dressed in military fatigues and the next as a Bedouin. Later in his career, he traveled with a staff of Ukrainian nurses and was protected by an all-female bodyguard cadre.

Even the Soviets thought Gaddafi was a little daffy, especially when he announced that Libya planned to join the Warsaw Pact. Needless to say, the Soviet Union never invited him to join the alliance, but they were more than happy to provide the small, oil-rich country with arms.

On August 19, 1981, Ronnie decided to test the Colonel by ordering American navy fighter jets to conduct an operation in the Gulf of Sidra, which Gaddafi claimed was Libyan territory. Two Libyan, Soviet-made jets attempted to intercept the Americans but were quickly shot down.

Ronnie successfully flexed American military muscle, showing the Libyan dictator just how badass the US Navy is, but Gaddafi was far from done.

The Berlin Bombing

Terrorism was fairly common in the 1980s, especially in Europe, but it was different in scope and character to what it is today. Most acts were carried out by left-wing groups—such as the Red Army Faction, the Red Brigades, Action Direct, and a host of others with names that sound like they were thought of by teenage boys—and although there were many and widespread, they usually didn't reach the casualty count of Islamist terrorist attacks today.

With that said, American military personnel in Europe, and sometimes even American bases, were constantly targeted by these groups.

Gaddafi made no secret that he supported many of these groups by providing them with arms and allowing members to train and live in Libya. The US already had sanctions on Libya by the time Reagan became president and as much as most Americans thought the guy was a psycho, those who knew of him didn't see him as much of a threat.

But then on April 5, 1986, a terrorist bomb ripped through a nightclub in West Berlin, West Germany, killing three, including a US serviceman. It was immediately believed that the nightclub was targeted because it catered to Americans. As American and West German police investigated, they revealed that Libyan intelligence agents, with the help of East German intelligence, had carried out the act.

Ronnie wasn't going to let this slide.

On April 15, 1986, Reagan ordered a massive air bombing attack on Libya. The jets left from an American base in Britain but were forced to avoid French, Spanish, and Italian territory on their way south. Still, the attack went through with the Americans only losing one jet and two men. Numerous Libyan communications facilities, airstrips, and other military installations were destroyed, but what made it a victory for Reagan and the Americans was Gaddafi's response.

Many Americans were braced for a series of terrorist attacks to hit the United States, or at least Americans overseas, but it never happened. Gaddafi ordered a missile attack on an American military institution in the Mediterranean, but the missiles famously missed by more than a mile. Although a passenger jet was blown up over Scotland in 1988, by terrorists who were years later connected to the Libyan government, Gaddafi never claimed responsibility for the attack.

In fact, after the bombing raid on Libya in 1986, Gaddafi didn't really say much of anything to or about the United States.

The Colonel had met his match!

Quotes about the Military

- "Of the four wars in my lifetime, none came about because the U.S. was too strong."

- "Your Bundeswehr is a model for the integration of defense needs with the democratic way of life. And you have not shrunk from the heavy responsibility of accepting the nuclear forces needed for deterrence." – in a June 9, 1982 address to the Bundestag in Bonn, West Germany.

- "If the Nazis during World War II and the Soviets today can recognize the Caribbean and Central America as vital to their interests, shouldn't we also?" – from the April 27, 1983 speech to Congress on Central America.

- "We do not deny any nation's legitimate interest in security. But protecting the security of one nation by robbing another of its national independence and national traditions is not legitimate. In the long run, it is not even secure." – as quoted in *The Quest for Peace, The Cause of Freedom*.

- "Above all, we must realize that no arsenal, or no weapon in the arsenals of our world, is so formidable as the will and moral courage of free men and women. It is a weapon our adversaries in today's world do not have."

CHAPTER 26

RISING ABOVE THE CHALLENGER DISASTER

Every notable leader in world history has faced unforeseen challenges that, more often than not, determined the course of their rule and how they were remembered in history. Effective leaders — true badasses, if you will — rose above these challenges and often used them to their advantage, demonstrating to their people the qualities of strength, tenacity, and perhaps most importantly, empathy.

Ronald Reagan had many unforeseen challenges come his way during his presidency, some of which we've already discussed — the Beirut bombing and the situation in Grenada, to name two — and at least one we'll get to a little later. But when the US Space Shuttle *Challenger* exploded in flames over the Atlantic Ocean on January 28, 1986, the American people were left reeling and confused over the tragedy, which ultimately helped define Reagan's second term as president.

How could this happen? Was this sabotage? Will we ever go into space again?

These questions and more were immediately asked by Americans from coast to coast in the aftermath of the incident.

That night, Reagan went on live television to address the nation. Although the reality of the tragedy didn't go away after Reagan's speech, Americans were put at ease and assured that life would continue.

Sending a Teacher into Space

NASA began the Space Shuttle program in 1981 as an easier and more efficient way to send astronauts into space. *Columbia* was the first Space Shuttle to make it into space in 1981 with *Challenger* being the second to go into service in 1983. The Space Shuttle program not only proved to be cost-effective for NASA, but it also brought renewed public interest to the agency. Crowds turned out to watch Space Shuttle launches from the Kennedy Space Center in Cape Canaveral, Florida, and becoming an astronaut was once again a popular desired occupation among children.

So, to take advantage of the public interest in space exploration, Ronnie announced the "Teacher in Space" program in 1984. After more than 11,000 applicants were screened, 37-year-old New Hampshire social studies teacher Christa McAuliffe was chosen to take the bold step to fly on the Space Shuttle *Challenger*. She would accompany Commander Francis Scobee, pilot Michael Smith, mission specialists Ronald McNair, Judith Resnik, and Ellison Onizuka, and payload specialist Gregory Jarvis.

But tragedy struck just over one minute after takeoff when the *Challenger's* O-rings failed, turning it into a fiery ball that fell in the ocean.

President Reagan was supposed to give his annual State of the Union Address that evening in front of Congress, but instead gave a more intimate address (written by Peggy Noonan) at the White House. With confidence and purpose, Reagan assured the American people that the disaster was more than likely an unfortunate accident (which turned out to be true). In a soft tone, he reassured the public that, together, life would get back to normal in the country.

The *Challenger* disaster defined the memories of many in Generation X, as more than 17% of all Americans watched the disaster on live TV, many of them schoolchildren. The disaster was never forgotten by the American people and remains a dark spot in American history, but thanks to the leadership of Ronald Reagan, Americans were able to get past more quickly and easily than might have been initially expected.

QUOTE ABOUT LEADERSHIP

- "The greatest leader is not necessarily the one who does the greatest things. He is the one that gets the people to do the greatest things."

- "What of all the entrepreneurs that fail? Well, many do, particularly the successful ones, often several times. And if you ask them the secret of their success, they'll tell you it's all that they learned in their struggles along the way. Yes, it's what they learned from failing." – from the address at Moscow State University on May 31, 1988.

- "If you think you can - you can!"

- "I was not a great communicator, but I communicated great things." – during the 1989 Farewell Address to the Nation.

- "Surround yourself with the best people you can find, delegate authority, and don't interfere as long as the policy you've decided upon is being carried out."

CHAPTER 27

I AM A CONTRA

As we've seen in this book, Ronnie was quite open about his war against communism; in fact, it was pretty much the main pillar of his foreign policy. Reagan's anti-communist philosophy was fairly popular with most Americans, although many in the Democrat Party believed that he was too much of a cowboy when it came to supporting some groups. For many Democrats, such as Ted Kennedy, the final straw was when Reagan proclaimed, "I am a Contra" when referring to the anti-communist guerrilla group in Nicaragua known as the Contras.

Kennedy, along with liberal Democratic Massachusetts Representative Edward Boland, devised a plan that would limit Reagan's support for the Contras, which became known as the "Boland Amendments." The Boland Amendments were three amendments to spending bills passed by both houses of Congress in 1982, 1983, and 1984, and signed by President Reagan. The amendments prohibited the US government from directly funding the Contras in their bid to overthrow the communist Sandinista government of Nicaragua. However, almost immediately, Reagan found workarounds.

The Boland Amendment wasn't going to stop Ronnie's anti-communist crusade.

Reagan allowed semi-covert CIA training camps to be established in Honduras and Guatemala, which skirted the limits of the Boland Amendments. The CIA claimed it wasn't giving arms or funds to the Contras, just minimal training and sanctuary.

The situation was allowed to stand until news of clear violations of the Boland Amendments became known. This was the biggest scandal of the Reagan administration and one of the most complex cases of espionage and arms dealing in modern history.

The Iran-Contra Affair

On November 3, 1986, an otherwise obscure Lebanese magazine called *Ash-Shiraa* published an unbelievable expose of arms deals taking place between countries that considered each other *persona non-grata*. The magazine stated that the American government was secretly shipping arms to the enemy state of Iran via Israel, which also saw Iran as an enemy. The arms shipments were part of a bigger deal whereby Iranian officials would convince their allies in the Shia militia Hezbollah to release Americans being held hostage in Lebanon. Israel would then be paid for its intermediary services.

If this situation wasn't bizarre and confusing enough to being with, it was further complicated when United States Marine Corps Lieutenant Colonel Oliver North became involved by suggesting that profits from the sales be funneled to the

Contras, which was in direct violation of the Boland Amendments.

Once the American press picked up the story, investigations and a hearing followed, leading to convictions of some Reagan administration officials for a number of crimes.

Nearly all were later pardoned when George H. W. Bush became president.

Ronnie at first denied knowing about the complex arms deals but later came clean. The reality is that the deals were so complex that he probably didn't know the extent of them. But it was certainly a major scandal, nonetheless, and not the way Reagan would have wanted to end his presidency. Actual weapons and arms were exchanged with enemies of the United States and laws were violated.

This was certainly much more of a scandal than a president having sexual relations with an intern or of a future president's advisor having a conversation with a Russian official during a campaign.

But 1987 was a different time and Reagan was certainly a different type of president. As an example of how badass Ronnie was, the American people didn't seem to care much about Iran-Contra. When he addressed the people after he was caught, Ronnie seemed sincere and contrite, assuring the public that he had probably been caught up in the heat of the moment. Besides, hostages were freed and the Contras aren't all bad if they're killing communists, right?

At least, that's what the majority of Americans thought when the details of the Iran-Contra Affair were publicized. If a scandal that big couldn't stop Reagan, nothing could.

Inspirational Reagan Quotes

- "I know in my heart that man is good. That what is right will always eventually triumph. And there's purpose and worth to each and every life."

- "We can't help everyone, but everyone can help someone."

- "Preparing for the future must begin, as always, with our children. We need to set for them new and more rigorous goals."

- "I don't believe in a fate that will fall on us no matter what we do. I do believe in a fate that will fall on us if we do nothing."

- "My philosophy of life is that if we make up our mind what we are going to make of our lives, then work hard toward that goal, we never lose – somehow we win out."

CHAPTER 28

"MR. GORBACHEV, TEAR DOWN THIS WALL!"

Ronald Reagan gave many speeches during his long and illustrious political career, but none were more forceful or meaningful than the one he gave on June 12, 1987, in front of the Berlin Wall. The Wall had been up for nearly 30 years at that point, separating democratic-capitalist West Berlin, West Germany from communist East Berlin, East Germany. The Wall had become the classic symbol of the Cold War and a physical example of the Iron Curtain that divided the communist East from the democratic West.

The Berlin Wall was also a Cold War flashpoint, being the scene of a near battle between Soviet and American troops when it was constructed by the communists, and was also where 239 people were killed by East German authorities as they tried to get to freedom in the West.

So, there is little doubt as to why Reagan chose that location to give his speech, but there is also little doubt as to why he chose to give that speech at that particular time.

On March 11, 1985, Mikhail Gorbachev became the leader of the Soviet Union, ushering in an era of unprecedented openness by the communist state. Gorbachev attempted to restructure the Soviet economy and bureaucracy through a program known as "perestroika" and allowed more freedom and civil liberties in what became known as "glasnost." For the first time in decades, Americans felt that maybe, just maybe, the Cold War may come to an end.

On December 8, 1987, Gorbachev and Reagan signed the Intermediate-Range Nuclear Forces Treaty, which called for a drastic reduction in both countries' nuclear arsenals. Reagan would go on to visit the Soviet Union and was asked there if he still believed the USSR was the evil empire, to which he replied, "I was talking about another time, another era."

Yes, by the time Ronald Reagan left the White House in January 1989, the Cold War was all but over, with the Americans victorious. McDonald's was in Moscow, the Berlin Wall was months away from coming down (but not before David Hasselhoff sang a tune on top of it!), the Warsaw Pact states would soon declare free elections, and by late 1991, even the Soviet Union dissolved.

Winning the Cold War

Historians and economists generally attribute many reasons for the collapse of the Soviet Union and communism in eastern Europe. Inherent weaknesses of the Soviet system are often pointed to as the primary reason, although what those weaknesses were are usually not clearly defined. Reagan himself often stated that the very ideas of communism and totalitarianism were so soul-crushing that it was inevitable that the people would eventually rise and demand a new system.

The reality is, though, that the primary weakness of the Soviet system was its economy.

Sure, Ronnie was opposed to the ideas of communism and totalitarianism and he knew that talking about them would play well for audiences around the world, but he really beat the communists by outspending. The Reagan Doctrine required large amounts of American dollars to fund anti-communist groups and governments around the world, and in response, the Soviets were required to dump an equal share of their rubles into their military, as well as communist governments and organizations around the world. In the end, the system of capitalism proved to be more efficient.

By the end of his second term, Reagan knew that he had won the Cold War, but in true badass fashion, he never gloated, nor did he brag. He simply offered advice to the Russian people about how to move forward in this new world and gave a little bit of hope to the rest of us that nuclear annihilation didn't have to be in our future.

QUOTES ABOUT PEACE

- "Strong and fundamental moral differences continue to exist between our nations but today on this vital issue, at least, we can see what can be accomplished when we pull together." – after the signing of the INF Treaty with Gorbachev on December 8, 1987.

- "It's time for us all, in the Middle East and around the world, to call a halt to conflict, hatred, and prejudice. It's time for us all to launch a common effort for reconstruction, peace, and progress." – September 1, 1982, television address to the nation about the Middle East.

- "But our strategy for peace with freedom must also be based on strength—economic strength and military strength."

- "Let's set the record straight. There is no argument over the choice between peace and war, but there is only one guaranteed way you can have peace and you can have it in the next second, 'surrender.'" – in his 1964 "Time for Choosing Speech."

- "For everyone, and above all, for our two great powers, the treaty whose text is on this table offers a big chance at last to get onto the road leading away from the threat catastrophe. It is our duty to take full advantage of that chance and to move together toward a nuclear free world which holds out for our children and grandchildren and for their children and grandchildren the promise of a fulfilling and happy life without fear and without a senseless waste of resources on weapons of destruction." – Remarks by Mikhail Gorbachev after the signing of the INF Treaty with Reagan on December 8, 1987.

CHAPTER 29

LEAVING OFFICE WITH A BADASS APPROVAL RATING

Ronnie was forced by the US Constitution to leave office after his second term, but when Vice President Bush won the 1988 presidential election, in many ways, it was the equivalent of a third term for Reagan. Massachusetts Governor Michael Dukakis was ahead in most of the polls going into September, by large margins in some, so briefly it seemed as though Americans had finally grown tired of Reagan. But when Bush ended up winning the election in a landslide, it affirmed that the 1980s were the decade of Reagan.

Reagan left office with a 68% approval rating, which is considered quite high; especially when one considers that the Iran-Contra Affair followed him out the door. But the reality is, the world and the United States were a much different place after Ronnie was through with them and most Americans were happy with the results.

Ronnie took office with the American economy in shambles, but by the time he left, the country had experienced one of its greatest periods of growth. The tech industry was starting to boom, home computers were becoming more common, average people were investing more and more in Wall Street, and most importantly, unemployment was fairly low. There was a renewed sense of optimism in America in 1989 that many people traced directly to Reagan.

Americans were also a lot less fearful in 1989 than they were in 1981. The Cold War was all but over and although the threat of nuclear annihilation wasn't totally gone, it didn't consume people's thoughts the way it once had. As Americans viewed their country generally more optimistically in 1989 than they had in 1981, so too did they view the world. Most Americans no longer saw the Russian people as bloodthirsty atheists who wanted to destroy their way of life but as people with many of the same hopes and dreams as themselves.

Changing some people's opinions is one thing, but changing the way millions of people view themselves, the world, and life is something else. Ronald Reagan accomplished that rare feat and for that, he is truly one of the United States' most badass presidents.

Quotes about History

- "Americans speak with the deepest reverence of those founding fathers and first citizens who gave us the freedoms that we enjoy today. And even though they lived over 200 years ago, we carry them in our hearts as well as our history books." – June 9, 1982 address to the Bundestag in Bonn, West Germany.

- "Looking back at the recent history of the world, I find it amazing how far civilization has retrogressed so quickly. As recently as World War I—granted the rules were violated at times—we had a set of rules of warfare in which armies didn't make war against civilians: Soldiers fought soldiers. Then came World War II and Hitler's philosophy of total war, which meant the bombing not only of soldiers but of factories that produced their rifles, and, if surrounding communities were also hit, that was to be accepted; then, as the war progressed, it became common for the combatants simply to attack civilians as part of military strategy. By the time the 1980s rolled around, we were placing our entire faith in a weapon whose fundamental target was the civilian population." – as quoted in *Ronald Reagan: An American Life*.

- "Not only did Margaret Thatcher and I become personal friends and share a similar philosophy about government; the alliance." – as quoted in *Ronald Reagan: An American Life*.

- "'Liberty has never come from government,' Woodrow Wilson, one of FDR's predecessors and another Democrat, said. 'The history of liberty is the history of limitation of government's power, not the increase of it.'" – as quoted in *Ronald Reagan: An American Life*.

- "At our one local movie theater, blacks and whites had to sit apart — the blacks in the balcony. My mother and father urged my brother and me to bring home our black playmates, to consider them equals, and to respect the religious views of our friends, whatever they were. My brother's best friend was black, and when they went to the movies, Neil sat with him in the balcony." – as quoted in *Ronald Reagan: An American Life*.

CHAPTER 30

PROTESTORS WERE NO MATCH FOR RONNIE

After handing the reins of power over to Bush, Ronnie and Nancy packed up their belongings in the White House and moved back to California. Reagan had done his service and now it was time for him to enjoy the fruits of his labor. The Reagans bought a large home in the swanky Bel-Air neighborhood of Los Angeles, although the couple also spent considerable time at their ranch.

Ronnie continued to make appearances on behalf of the Republican Party well into the 1990s, but his age was slowing him down and in 1994, he was diagnosed with Alzheimer's disease. Still, an interesting incident took place in 1992 that demonstrated Reagan was still a badass, even at the age of 81!

On April 13, 1992, Reagan was in Las Vegas, Nevada to accept an award from the National Association of Broadcasters for his work in early radio. Just after Reagan accepted the two-foot high crystal eagle statue, an anti-nuclear protester posing as a reporter grabbed the award and smashed it. As soon as the incident happened, Secret Service officers leaped into action and arrested the man, but Ronnie didn't seem very fazed by the events. Reagan just smiled and walked off the stage.

There's no way a crazed protester could be any match for Reagan!

Unfortunately, though, no matter how badass Reagan was, he could not beat Alzheimer's disease. His son Ronald believes that the disease may have been showing its signs for several years, but by 1994, its grip on the fortieth president was undeniable. Ronnie knew that it was only a matter of time before his once sharp mind was forever gone, so he wrote a sort of farewell letter to the American people in November 1994. Part of it read:

> "I now begin the journey that will lead me into the sunset of my life. I know that for America there will always be a bright dawn ahead. Thank you, my friends. May God always bless you."

Reagan's condition continued to deteriorate and although he spent his final few years in relative isolation, he never forgot who Nancy was. Finally, on June 5, 2004, Ronald Reagan died from pneumonia at the age of 93 in his Los Angeles, California home. He was buried on the grounds of his ranch near Santa Barbara, which now serves as the Ronald Reagan Presidential Library and Museum.

That many world leaders, including Gorbachev, and members of the Democrat Party attended his official, state funeral, is a testament to Ronald Reagan's status as a true badass leader who earned the respect of his adversaries throughout his lifetime.

Some Rapid-Fire Badass Reagan Quotes

- "Like a chrysalis we're emerging from the economy of the industrial revolution, an economy confined to and limited by the Earth's physical resources, into as one economist titled his book, the "economy in mind," in which there are no bounds on human imagination and the freedom to create is the most precious natural resource." – address to Russian college students at Moscow State University on May 31, 1988.

- "Christmas can be celebrated in the school room with pine trees, tinsel and reindeers, but there must be no mention of the man whose birthday is being celebrated. One wonders how a teacher would answer if a student asked why it was called Christmas."

- "You can tell a lot about a fellow's character by his way of eating jellybeans."

- "You repeat that at every meeting!" – Gorbachev to Reagan at the signing of the INF Treaty with Gorbachev on December 8, 1987, after Reagan stated, "Trust but Verify" in Russian.

- "Heroes may not be braver than anyone else. They're just braver five minutes longer."

CONCLUSION

Ronald Reagan was truly a man and a president for his time. He probably wouldn't have been elected if he had come along a little earlier. It's also not likely that he would have won the highest office in the land if he arrived on the scene a few years later. Reagan was the man America needed when the chips were down, and he possessed the sort of spirit and attitude that Americans loved in the 1980s: he was rough, tough, and he was taking names.

Truly, Ronald Reagan lived his life as a badass — from his days in Hollywood to the governorship of California, and finally, as President of the United States of America — Ronnie exuded confidence in all his decisions, even those he later regretted, such as the Iran-Contra Affair. Reagan used his badass speaking abilities to connect to the American people and his badass leadership style to win countless political battles, but it was his badass attitude toward communism in general and the Soviet Union in particular for which he's best remembered.

As World War II ended, the specter of another potential world war gripped the planet, and by the 1960s, it was clear that if World War III ever did happen, it could be the end of modern civilization. Different American presidents had very different strategies for dealing with the Cold War, from appeasement to containment, but Reagan decided to face the threat head-on.

When Ronald Reagan became president, he made it very clear that he was going to be the president who won the Cold War. Many thought Reagan was out of his mind or just talking big for votes, but by the time he left office in 1989, it was apparent that he *would* be remembered as the president who won the Cold War. But as badass as that may be, the fact that he did it while losing a minimum number of Americans puts him on another level of badassness. Yes, American lives were lost in combat during Reagan's two terms as president, but the numbers were far lower than the casualties seen during the presidencies of George W. Bush and even Barack Obama.

Ultimately, Ronald Reagan is remembered as one of the United States' most popular and effective post-World War II presidents. Sure, he had some problems and things didn't always go the way the fortieth president wanted but saving the American economy and ending the Cold War have placed him in a category with few other American presidents. Needless to say, they are all badasses just like Reagan!

DON'T FORGET YOUR FREE BOOKS

GET THEM FOR FREE ON
WWW.TRIVIABILL.COM

MORE BOOKS BY BILL O'NEILL

I hope you enjoyed this book and learned something new.

Please feel free to check out some of my previous books on Amazon.

Printed in Great Britain
by Amazon